THE
UY
RANCH
Reminiscences of a
Montana Stockman's Wife, 1912-1921

THE UY RANCH

Reminiscences of a
Montana Stockman's Wife, 1912-1921

Helen Addison Howard

Sunflower University Press®
1531 Yuma (Box 1009), Manhattan, Kansas 66502-4228 USA

© 1989 by Helen Addison Howard

ISBN 0-89745-123-6

Edited by Ginger Weir

Index by Terry G. Colbert

Layout by Lori L. Daniel

*In Memoriam to
my lifelong friend,
Dorothy B. Taylor
1903-1982*

Contents

Preface ix

Chapter 1 — Arrival in Montana — 1912 1

Chapter 2 — Spring Roundup and Carrie's
Betrothal — 1912 13

Chapter 3 — Episodes on a Sheep Ranch — 1912 27

Chapter 4 — Trials and Tribulations of a Country
Schoolma'am — 1912-1913 37

Chapter 5 — A Dashing Lochinvar and Showdown
with Sadie — 1912-1913 53

Chapter 6 — The UY's Colorful Boss 67

Chapter 7 — Carrie's Wedding and Rangeland
Violence — 1913 79

Chapter 8 — Plight of the Nesters — 1914-1915 93

Chapter 9 — A Lonely, Youthful Wayfarer —
1914-1916 107

Chapter 10 — Mystery of Bill Solved — 1916 115

Chapter 11 — An Elopement and More
Violent Crises — 1916-1917 127

Chapter 12 — New Catastrophes — 1918-1919 143

Chapter 13 — The Tragic Drought — 1919-1920 155

Chapter 14 — The Aftermath of the
Drought — 1921 163

Epilogue 170

Genealogical Chart 181

Appendices 182

Index 189

Preface

In 1933 a mutual friend in Los Angeles introduced me to Carrie Cather Lucas, because we both were former Montanans — she from near Miles City in eastern Montana, and I a native of Missoula in western Montana. Carrie told my friend, Leona, and me some highlights of her eventful ranch life between 1913 and 1921, and I began taking notes of her oral history during a summer series of interviews in 1934.

Carrie — or "Pat" as Leona and I knew her — was then married to American Expeditionary Forces (AEF) veteran Val Lucas, who was dying of tuberculosis from gassed lungs in World War I. Because Val objected to Carrie recalling UY Ranch days with her first husband, she left a great many gaps in her reminiscences, particularly in the later phases, and was vague about many specifics. I lost touch with Carrie — or Pat — in 1935, so that the first-person, sketchy narrative manuscript remained forgotten in my files.

Meanwhile, world travel occupied my time and interest. Between globe-trotting jaunts, I researched material for my first Western Americana book, *War Chief Joseph*. Two more Western histories followed in 1963 and 1965, and a paperback reprint of *Saga of Chief Joseph* (Bison Books, 1978). After publication of *American Indian Poetry* in September 1979, an ethnohistory, literary critique, and *American Frontier Tales* scheduled for fall 1980 but postponed until January 1982, 1980 seemed an auspicious time to complete the factual history of UY Ranch life, mostly from a woman's viewpoint. Stockmen and homesteaders in the 1912 to 1921 years had become historical figures who lived during the transition of the old to the new West. These people were not the stereotypes found in the movies and popular fiction. They were real people confronting real problems in a developing region, which gave insights into the actualities — the dreams, joys, and tragedies — of Western life.

Therefore, the book's scope should be broadened from the personal account of Carrie and her husband, boss of the UY Ranch, to include an informative, objective tribute to eastern Montana's stockmen, sheepmen, and homesteaders, all of whom contributed to the settlement, stock raising, and agricultural development of the Treasure State. Moreover, the enlarged context of rural dwellers in general would enrich the historical perspective by providing documentary information concerning ranching and farming during the years 1913-1921 on Miles City's "north side" in the Sunday Creek area, of which there seems to be a significant void in published books.

Accomplishing these individual and general goals and filling in and authenticating gaps in the personal story have required documentation from a variety of primary sources. One of the first steps was to verify certain biographical facts about Earl W. "Smokey" Nichols through his death certificate, marriage and divorce records relating to his first wife, last will and testament, property inventory and appraisement, and District Court trials involving him as plaintiff and defendant. Contemporary newspapers are also a mother-lode informational source for the serious historian. Microfilms of these were furnished by the Montana Historical Society Library. During the 1980 summer, I examined, page by page, microfilms of the *Independent* and the *Yellowstone Journal* for the year 1901; *Independent* for 1915-1919 inclusive; *American* for 1913-1917 inclusive; *Star* for 1913-1917 inclusive; and the Miles City *American and Stockgrowers*

Journal, 1917-1918 inclusive. The years skipped prior to 1913 were irrelevant to Carrie's and Smokey's ranch life together, the chief focus of the book.

Obviously, much material had to be quoted verbatim from official documents and news media to substantiate without bias the recorded facts, and thereby obviate any impressions or erroneous beliefs on the part of relatives or friends that the persons named had been unfairly or inaccurately presented. Of value also were interviews, by telephone or letter, of the subjects' contemporaries — relatives, neighbors, friends, acquaintances.

Other sources consulted were *Before Barbed Wire*, by Mark Brown and W. R. Felton (Bramhall House, New York, 1956); *A Bride Goes West*, by Nannie Alderson and Helena Huntington Smith (Farrar and Rinehart, New York, 1942); *Golden Fleece*, by Hughie Call (Houghton Mifflin Co., Boston, 1942); *Free Grass to Fences*, by Robert H. Fletcher (published for the Montana Historical Society by the University Press, 1969); "Henry Sieben: Pioneer Montana Stockman," by Dick Pace, in *Montana, the Magazine of Western History* (Montana Historical Society, Helena, January 1979); "Journal of a Ranch Wife: 1932-1935," edited by Helen Crosby Glenn, in *Frontier and Midland* (Montana State University, Missoula, Summer 1939); *Montana; an Uncommon Land*, by K. Ross Toole (University of Oklahoma Press, Norman, 1959); "Montana Episodes: Shipping Time," edited by Jeffrey J. Safford, in *Montana, the Magazine of Western History* (Montana Historical Society, Helena, April 1979); *Not in Precious Metals Alone; a Manuscript History of Montana*, compiled and edited by the staff of the Montana Historical Society (Helena, 1976), First Edition; "Sollid Wants to See You: George Sollid, Homestead Locator," by William E. Farr, in *Montana, the Magazine of Western History* (Montana Historical Society, Helena, April 1979); and "Vigorous Attempts to Prosecute: Pinkerton Men on Montana's Range, 1914," by Joan Bishop, in *Montana, the Magazine of*

Western History (Montana Historical Society, Helena, April 1980).

From this combination of researched material, after applying both inductive and deductive methods, evaluating the sources by cross-checking with various references wherever necessary, I hope that the facts of history have emerged in an accurate, fair, objective, and unbiased manner. Errors of fact may be found by some knowledgeable readers because of misinformation given by informants at this date 68 years later, or because of their lack of knowledge about specifics. It is my hope, though, that readers will be enlightened and entertained by this historical account of eastern Montana people, their times, and their environment.

The reminiscences, as Carrie recalled them in our interviews, have been edited for clarity, conciseness, and continuity. Some of her recollections are recorded in her own words.

I must emphasize that this is essentially Carrie's story as I never knew her sister, Elsie, personally.

Past experience has acquainted me with the problems, realities, and vicissitudes of ranchers and homesteaders. As a child, I camped with my parents in the upper Bitter Root Valley on the Nez Perce Fork, locally called "the West Fork," of the Bitter Root River near a cattle ranch where I played with the rancher/farmer's young daughter and son; joined in their chores; learned to milk cows, drive a team of horses hitched to a single plow, and keep a furrow straight; and even attended their one-room log schoolhouse. Later, my lifelong friend and college chum, Dorothy Taylor of Missoula, and I spent a summer on her Uncle Arthur Gill's horse ranch on Little Tongue River, 27 miles northwest of Sheridan, Wyoming, and about a mile from Dayton. In 1932, I sojourned at Dorothy's homestead on Little Powder River, a half-mile north of the Wyoming state line where Dorothy had taught at the Biddle School a few years before filing and proving up on her homestead. Her nearby cattle ranching neighbors were the Drexels. Mr. Drexel had emigrated from Saxony in southern Germany. In the vicinity, I met Bob

Fudge, ex-cowboy and gentleman of the old school who still retained his Texas drawl. He had trailed north with the longhorns in the early days to the XIT Ranch located near the Hat X on Timber Creek near the Big Dry, south of the Missouri River.

As a cub reporter/feature writer on Missoula's *Daily Missoulian* while still a teenage high school senior (and continuing during four university years and for two years after graduation, until I moved to California in 1929), I was assigned in the summer of 1923 to the Missoula Tourist Camp up Rattlesnake Creek to get news or features. I interviewed a few wealthy tourists from the Atlantic Coast, but mostly the host of penniless homesteaders who were migrating with a few scant possessions in their Model T Ford touring cars from their drought-ridden acres in central and eastern Montana to seek work in the apple orchards around Spokane or the Seattle shipyards.

In conclusion, then, *The UY Ranch* is a composite real-life story of the real West, told "like it was," beginning with Carrie's arrival in Montana to visit her homesteading married sister, Elsie, near Westmore.

An unhappy Midwestern teenager with a stern, domineering father, Carrie was determined to escape his stifling influence. She had become infused with the Western fiction novelists' romantic ideals of ranch life, and she wanted to be a pioneer. A romance with her sister's husband's younger brother added to the excitement of new experiences. To sever her economic dependence on her father, Carrie got her first job teaching in a country school, which meant separation for the lovers. When the engagement ended in bitter heartbreak, Carrie's marriage to the UY Ranch boss seemed to be the answer to her romantic dreams.

But the cruelty of nature on the range, with its long, cold winters compounded by the harsher realities of the homesteaders' or "nesters' " lifestyle, the violence caused by the conflict of cattle, horse, and sheep interests, great stock losses because of years of drought, and declining prices for livestock, resulting in economic ruin for thousands of homesteaders and ranchers alike, caused Carrie's hair to turn white by the time she was 27 and might have destroyed her sanity if she had not learned to close a door of her mind to yesterday and look forward to tomorrow as another day, a fresh start. The glamour was gone, yet she never lost her sense of humor in retrospect, and the maturity she gained sustained her through many future years of good and bad fortunes. Nor did the Montana range and its friendly Western people ever lose their appeal for her, despite the fact that the Western experience had metamorphosed her from a shy, timid, romantic girl into a self-assertive, at times quarrelsome, woman, which caused animosities with friends and relatives, some of which were never resolved.

It is with deep gratitude that I acknowledge the invaluable help and assistance of the following persons, in alphabetical rather than meritorious order: Bruce M. Brown, Brown and Huss Law Offices, Miles City, Montana; Tom Colleran, Secretary, Range Riders Museum, Miles City; Mrs. Muriel D. Cooksey, Director, Miles City Public Library; Miss Linda L. Hieb, Reference Librarian, Miles City Public Library; Walter E. Mann, Ogden, Utah; Montana Department of Health and Environmental Sciences, Bureau of Records and Statistics, Helena; Bruce T. Mott, Miles City; the late Mrs. Carrie Cather Nichols, Los Angeles; Mrs. Margaret Mann Nichols, San Francisco; Don Pering, Miles City; Bob Petrucco, Reference Staff, Burbank Public Library; Don Pyle, Miles City; Mrs. Norah Nichols Randolph, San Francisco; Range Rider Reps, Mrs. Maurice Fleming, President, and the Executive Board of Miles City, for their kind permission to use material from *Fanning the Embers*; Mrs. Margaret Reid, Deputy Clerk, District Court, Custer County, Miles City; Hal Ross, Coffrin's Old West Gallery, Miles City; Mrs. Ernest Schwabenthal, Chico, California; Dave Walter, Reference Librarian, Montana Historical Society Library, Helena.

In addition, Smokey's granddaughter, Betty Grayce Nichols (Mrs. David Kalfell), El Toro, California, and Smokey's grandson, Paul Nichols, Sunburst, Montana, have earned a special debt of gratitude — Betty Grayce for supplying various family photos, her brother Paul for his enthusiastic response to the project. Also, I am indebted for other family photos and rare scenes of Smokey Nichols' UY-Rafter T horse ranch activities kindly loaned me by Mrs. Margaret Mann Nichols ("Bub" Nichols' widow), San Francisco, California, and by her brother, Walter E. Mann, Ogden, Utah.

Helen Addison Howard
Burbank, California

Chapter 1

Arrival in Montana

As the train clickety-clacked over the snow-swept Montana prairie, Carrie Cather congratulated herself that she had finally stood up to her father and made the big decision to leave home. At eighteen she would make her own way in the world and become both economically and socially independent. All the resentment that had festered in her during years of growing up under paternal domination had boiled over in rebellion. Her father was more strict with her than a prison warden. Reading, she recalled, was one pleasure he had never forbidden. Nor, in fairness to him, had he ever objected to hauling her precious books from their Wisconsin farm in autumn to the house he rented in town so that she might have the advantages of a high school education. But he never let her go to parties, have dates with boys, or any special chums with girls.

Carrie remembered the good times her ten brothers and sisters enjoyed while they were growing up. They were all married and scattered throughout the country now. Being youngest, she was the last one at home.

"My father," she declared, "had resolved to keep me there, not by gently coercing me but by sheer domination. Denied social life, I had become more shy and awkward than ever, but I was content to study. I still loved my books and my dreams."

Carrie remembered with affection her gray-haired mother, who had the weatherbeaten skin of a farm woman. Her mother's kindly sympathy made up for the stern qualities in her father's character. Through her mother's understanding and intercession, Carrie got her father's permission to visit a sister.

"I had decided to come to my sister's homestead because my father's dominating influence had begun to smother me, and I wanted to get away, just anywhere. I'd saved money from the sale of sheep I'd raised on the farm the last summer. That little more than paid expenses to Sis' and George Griffith's place. If I'd had money enough, I would have gone to Colorado where an older brother and sister lived. Ever since Sis — that's Elsie — moved to Montana though, she'd been writing me, her youngest sister, to 'come out to see us.'"

As the train slowed for her stop, Carrie stared fascinated out the car window at the snowy plain extending to the horizon. Drenched in moonlight, its blue-white vastness filled her with awe and with a sense of freedom and adventure. All the old unhappiness was now behind her. Gone was her feeling of frustration, of being held down by parental control. Out here, she felt deeply, a new life would soon unfold. Oh, the wonder and joy of it!

Although she left home two days after a severe March blizzard, she didn't hear the merciless wind tearing across the prairie like a million howling demons of destruction, its frozen breath bringing suffering and death to cattle and sheep. She saw only the rangeland's crystalline beauty, sparkling like myriads of diamonds in the blue-white moonlight.

The train jerked to a stop at a siding. In the vestibule, Carrie gathered her ankle-length skirts and leaped from the steps into a foot of snow. Cold air hit like icy water dashed in her face. She gasped and raised the coat's fur collar about her neck. The brakeman handed down her two suitcases, advising her to "keep well wrapped up." Clutching one in either mittened hand, she glanced around in bewilderment at a collection of low buildings. Huddled darkly on the snowfield, they appeared to be still

Chapter 1 — Arrival in Montana

cowering from the storm's vengeance. Westmore was a typical Western town, she learned later, a couple of general stores and saloons, and perhaps a half-dozen houses scattered haphazardly along the tracks over the countryside. The train puffed out clouds of steam and, clanging and grinding, rumbled away into the moonlit night.

Carrie had time only to glimpse her surroundings before two bulky figures came towards her. She smiled in relief. They would be sister Elsie and her husband George. She dropped the suitcases into the snow as the smaller figure cried out in Sis' excited voice, "Oh, Carrie, it's so good to see you again!" Sis hugged her to the padded bosom of a sheepskin-lined coat. Then she turned to her tall companion, also bundled up to the ears in a sheepskin coat, and announced, "Surprise! This is Billy, George's kid brother."

He muttered shyly, "Pleased to meetcha," and pulled off a woolly mitten.

Carrie grasped a warm, sinewy hand which gripped hers in a hearty clasp. That act sealed their friendship, for she felt instantly attracted to this young man. Sis had an arm around her waist and was saying, "George's working on a sheep ranch to earn spare cash, so Billy's looking after things."

Bill still held Carrie's hand, staring in candid admiration into her eyes. She felt her sister stiffen, although she paid no heed at the time to the movement.

"Well," Sis said, "you two goin' to hold hands while we freeze to death? Come on, let's hightail to the bobsled." She gave them a peculiar glance and strode away, plowing her way through the snow.

Carrie felt the blood rush to her face. Bill quickly released her hand and stooped to pick up the suitcases. That queer look of Sis', which Carrie took as jealousy, was puzzling to her. Was it just Sis' lack of tact? She trailed in silent confusion after Sis, whose long skirts dragged along the white path. Hard, dry, powdery snow crystals creaked under their shoes with startling clarity in the frosty air.

As though nothing untoward had happened, Sis tucked her snugly in warm hay in the sled bottom. Bill tossed in the luggage and hunched down in front of the girls. He clucked to the team of shaggy black horses and they started along Westmore's deserted street for the homestead. Hitchrails, Carrie noticed, stood before the darkened post office and general store, blacksmith shop and livery barn. In 1912 horses were used more often than automobiles. Lamplight cast squares of yellow light through dingy saloon windows on the snowy street where a few saddled horses stood humped and tied to the rail.

Soon they had passed the last frame building. Under Bill's urging the black team trotted steadily for mile after mile over the moonlit plain, harness jingling and sled runners squeaking on the hard-packed snow. It was a lonesome drive with no tree, house, or light in sight, but the prairie vastness filled Carrie with a kind of fearful joy. Stars in the sky's dark blue dome sparkled through icily clear air.

They traveled so far in the wintry wilderness that it seemed to Carrie they would be in Dakota before long, though she wasn't sure in what direction they were headed.

"Sis asked me innumerable questions about Mother and Dad, our brothers and sisters, and old friends back home on the farm. Bill drove in silence; even if he wanted to, he couldn't have squeezed a word in edgeways through Sis' eager chatter. The cold became sharper with each succeeding mile. My legs grew cramped to numbness, and the polar air seeped through my clothing. Tingling chills coursed down into my vitals. I was forced to hold a mittened hand over my nose to keep it from freezing."

Just as she began thinking she could bear it no longer, a light gleamed suddenly beside the road, which paralleled a barbed wire fence. She could make out a man's form holding a lantern by a gate. As they drew abreast of him, he called out a cheery, "Howdy, Bill and Elsie."

Bill pulled up the horses, and Sis asked if anything was the matter.

"Oh, no. Ma sent me down to tell yuh she's got a hot supper waitin' for all of yuh."

"Bless her, that's sure kind of her!" Sis glanced at Carrie. "I guess a hot meal will thaw out our tenderfoot here." She introduced her sister to Worden Vandervoort, who was about twenty, short, and thickset.

"Howdy," he acknowledged Carrie's formal, "I'm pleased to meet you." He blew out the lantern and jumped into the sled, squeezing in beside Bill.

They turned through the gate and followed a snow-laden truck winding down a "draw" or coulee for a quarter mile or more, Carrie judged, to a small, tarpaper-covered house. Two shaggy dogs rushed out barking furiously, but at a word from Worden low whines replaced their challenge. The sled stopped near the door. Carrie got stiffly to her feet, clambered over the side, and stamped about in the snow to restore her circulation.

Sis led the way to the doorstep, while the boys drove off in the sled.

"The moment I stepped into the Vandervoort's homestead shack its spotlessness struck me. A large room housed the plainest of furniture, but rag rugs on the much-scrubbed board floor gave it a homey air. As my mother would have said, 'Everything had a place, and everything was in its place.' "

Mrs. Vandervoort had a curious but friendly stare in her pale blue eyes and was wiping her right hand on her apron as she came forward to greet Carrie. Small and chubby like her two sons, she had the ruddy complexion of the Dutch.

"My lands," she said in a hearty voice, "we've heard so much about you from Elsie seem's if we'd known you right along. And you're just as purty as the boys surmised."

Carrie blushed and murmured something that sounded appropriate, she hoped.

Worden and Bill, stamping snow from their boots, came in from the barn where they had made the horses comfortable. While Bill greeted his hostess, Worden carried a chair for Carrie over by the kitchen stove.

Mrs. Vandervoort turned to Carrie again and said in the big-hearted way that all westerners seemed to have, "Now you just sit right down there and get yourself toasted. You must be half froze alive, child. Land's sake, I never did see such a long, cold winter. Take off your coat and be comfortable, and the vittles will be served in a minute." She went back to the range and bustled about amid a clatter of pots and pans, meanwhile chatting with Sis.

The appetizing odor of good, wholesome food cooking floated in a steamy vapor throughout the room. Suddenly Carrie became aware of sharp, insistent hunger pains gnawing at her stomach, as the room's moist heat soaked through her, making her drowsy. She felt ravenous enough to relish cowhide.

The boys sat at some distance from the stove, while Sis moved from table to cupboard shelves, setting the places with the familiarity that comes from friendship. It was Carrie's first opportunity to observe Bill, her brother-in-law's younger brother, whom she guessed to be her own age. She described him as: "Like a romantic cowboy out of fiction he was, handsome, six feet tall, although he seemed at a loss what to do with hands and feet. He kept putting his hands in his pockets, thrusting his feet out in front of him and drawing them back beneath the chair. He had those very expressive kind of brown eyes, soft, chestnut-brown hair and copper-tan skin, and oh, such a lovable disposition hidden under his natural shyness. Already I felt a tingle whenever he glanced at me in that friendly, though boyishly embarrassed kind of way he had." She laughed happily at the memory.

Bill exchanged a comment now and then with Worden and his older brother. Carrie was aware, though, that he kept eyeing sidelong her city clothes and slender figure, and that his eyes lingered on her mass of short, black curls.

"How's Peggy?" she heard him ask Worden. His voice, although resonant, was soft and low.

"Oh, she's fine."

So bashful Worden had a girl. She wondered if Bill had a

Chapter 1 — Arrival in Montana

sweetheart, and hoped he didn't. As a friendly overture, she overcame her own shyness, looked directly at Bill, and asked if he had lived out West long.

He replied that George brought him out last summer. Prompted by further questioning, he said he was from Wisconsin and was going to high school. When asked whether he liked Montana, he said he guessed it was all right but he missed the trees.

Carrie declared that the hardwood forests back home seemed like prisons to her, they "shut you in so." She liked the open range country.

Sis interposed on her way to the table, arms full of dishes, that she'd have Billy play his guitar and sing cowboy songs "when we get to our shack."

Flustered at being the object of attention, Bill, with a self-conscious grin, shuffled his feet and ducked his head. "Aw," he protested, from a wryly twisted mouth, "I don't sing; I only make a noise."

Sis gently chided him as she put down the dishes, "Now, Billy, don't go runnin' yourself down." She went over to him and ran her fingers through his hair, ruffling it in a rather possessive way. Carrie thought the gesture overly familiar.

"Grub's on!" interrupted Mrs. Vandervoort. "Draw up the chairs, Worden. Come on, Carrie, and eat while it's hot."

Carrie needed no urging to take her place at the table next to Sis, for the savory aroma of an old-fashioned country dinner steaming hot from the kitchen range had been tantalizing her ever since she entered the house. The hands of the alarm clock on the shelf above the stove, she noticed, pointed to nine. Mrs. Vandervoort served her generous portions of baked beans, stewed chicken and dumplings, and canned tomatoes. Sis brought out of the oven a pan of golden-brown biscuits, and then poured each one a cup of strong coffee. All fell silent, devoted to the business of eating. The food, seasoned just enough, tasted like no other Carrie had ever eaten, so keenly had the wintry air whetted her appetite.

"Everything went along nicely," Carrie recalled, "until Mrs. Vandervoort, in her outspoken way, made a vulgar remark about the meal that caused me to blush to my toenails. Later, after I became acquainted with the country, I realized that the incident was a typical contrast of this land — open, warmhearted generosity often expressed in a glaring, crude way — a strange mixture."

Immediately after Sis had helped Mrs. Vandervoort with the dishes, the guests took their leave. Fortified by hot food, the drive in the sub-zero temperature didn't seem half so cold or so long to Carrie, although the Vandervoort place was about halfway to Sis' homestead. Carrie snuggled into the hay and listened to the not unmusical jingle of harness on the trotting horses, and to the hissing of the snow under the sled's runners.

Suddenly, Sis nudged her and pointed, "Look!"

Far off to the left a coyote sat atop a knoll. Nose pointing to the moon and brilliant stars, he voiced a long-drawn howl, echoing across the snow-smothered plain. Infinitely sad, it sounded like the wail of a lonely spirit, yet it quickened the pace of Carrie's blood.

Intuitively in that moment, she felt she had become bone and tissue of this land; that she would grow and develop with it, laugh with it, suffer with it, and oh, how she'd live in its mighty vigorousness! The severity of its winter storms would mold her character in its own stern lines, and the burning heat of its summer sun would harden her in the fierce struggle to survive.

"I had come of good Anglo-Irish pioneer stock — as near as I could gather from the little my father told. We were a race of pioneers — the God-fearing, law-abiding kind that give stability to any new land, and these principles had been instilled into us from childhood. We were one branch of a fine old Virginia family whose daughter Willa Cather was making the name famous in American letters. Even in my earliest dreams I wanted to go into new country where life was untamed and feel the exciting thrill of the conqueror. Now I felt my desires would be fulfilled in this land still unconquered by youth. The thought

Chapter 1 — Arrival in Montana

that there would be agony — hardship, disappointment, heartbreak — along with the ecstasy didn't enter my young mind."

It must have been past midnight, she guessed, when they reached Sis' homestead after entering rolling prairie country, for the moon was waning. Like most of the shacks, her place was a box-like frame one, although George had built it all of hardwood which he had shipped west. It stood boldly along the edge of a little, wooded coulee that separated the house from the barns. While Bill stabled the horses the girls went inside.

After Sis lighted the lamp, Carrie observed that one huge room accommodated all the needs of living quarters. As she glanced around, she saw a kitchen range in one corner, and opposite it a large, square table covered by a checkered oilcloth. At the room's far end two double beds occupied either corner. Too tired to notice further details, she blurted, "Do we have to undress out in the open?"

Sis laughed heartily at her sister's delicate fears as she hung her coat on a nail in the board wall. "Course not, you silly. We draw these around, and presto, we've got two bedrooms." She began pulling figured calico curtains on wires to block off the beds. "You sleep in this bed with me because Billy uses the other one." She gave Carrie a mischievous look. "You don't sleepwalk, do you?"

"Certainly not!" Carrie blushed, hating her shy awkwardness. She hoped to overcome it now that she had started out in the world on her own.

So deeply buried within her that she was only half conscious of it, she envied her older sister's ready tongue. She could never think of the right answer at the right time. But Carrie intimated she was aware of other contrasts favorable to her. Sis, taller and larger boned than she was, had a plain face and brown hair which she braided and coiled around her head. Her dark eyes often mirrored a sly, teasing look that could quickly change to one of sharpness. Carrie, though, knew that her own regular features were considered pretty in a demure, prim sort of way. Quiet among strangers, she could be vivacious around girls her own age, but among boys her shy aloofness failed to attract them.

While hurriedly taking off her clothes in the bitterly cold air, Carrie said between chattering teeth to hide her confusion, that Bill seemed "awfully nice."

Sis shrugged and pulled off her dress. "Oh, he's useful around here to do the chores while George's away."

As Sis stepped out of her petticoat, Carrie noticed an unusual fullness about her figure. Catching the glance, Sis said in pretended disappointment, "Big Eyes, you've already discovered my surprise. Yes, I'm expecting sometime in the fall. If it's a girl I'll name her 'Carrie' after you."

Noting the mischievous twinkle in her sister's eyes, Carrie made a wry face.

Quickly slipping into a long, flannel nightgown, Sis buttoned it, and then hugged Carrie, who sat on the bed's edge in thoughtful silence.

In an exultant voice, Sis admitted, "Now you know why I was so tickled to have you come out at this time. You'll be able to help me a lot with the cooking and sewing. And it won't seem so lonesome with another girl around. You'll stay all summer, won't you?"

"As long as I'm welcome. You know how it is at home. I didn't tell the folks, but I hoped I could get a job out here — teaching school, maybe. I've only got ten dollars, but it'll help with the groceries."

"You silly goose," Sis told her, "you save your money. You'll need it to help you get a job."

As Carrie slipped between the icy cold blankets that had the soapy smell of home laundering, she wondered what had prompted Sis to make such a disparaging remark about Bill — in strange contrast to the affectionate way she spoke to him at the Vandervoorts'.

After Sis slid in beside her and their combined bodily heat warmed the bed, Carrie relaxed and drifted into a doze with a happier feeling than she had known for a long time. Sis, Carrie recalled, had been married in 1908 to George Griffith, who had grown up in Wisconsin. He had taken a job as errand boy, and finally as a salesman in the local department store. Sis had graduated before Carrie, being older, and had begun clerking in the dry goods department. There Sis had met George. Carrie had known her sister had a beau, but never met him until he and Sis were married. This had seemed rather strange, although she never analyzed Sis' motive. George, Sis had confided to her, was unhappy and wanted to return to the country. From traveling salesmen, he had heard about free land in 1909, open to homestead entry on the cattle ranges of eastern Montana. About two years after their marriage they had filed on a grazing claim in 1910, seventy miles southeast of Miles City.

  Carrie felt doubly grateful for Sis' oft-repeated invitations to "come West and be a cowgirl." There were plenty of good-looking cowpunchers on the loose and roaming the country, Sis promised. Now, here she was, and she had already met a young homesteader-turned-cowboy. Again she experienced an odd feeling of certainty that an eventful new life was about to begin. And Bill's image was the last impression to fade from her sleepy mind.

Chapter 2

Spring Roundup and Carrie's Betrothal 1912

Three weeks later, it seemed to Carrie, spring appeared overnight. First came a chinook wind from the west, imparting a peculiar bluish clarity to the air and melting snow on butte tops and south slopes between sunrise and sunset. During the thawing period every ravine and gully ran full of roily water. Through bare patches of muddy ground, the range burst forth in a carpet of succulent green grass. The first wildflowers of blue crocus, yellow buttercup, and purple shooting-star nodded their gaily colored blooms to chill April winds. Meadowlarks sang brief melodious notes from the sagebrush; grouse or prairie chicken cocks began to sound their hollow booming mating call. Soon frisky calves and foals were getting acquainted in ludicrous fashion with long, awkward legs. Amid all this new life, Carrie felt a buoyant uplifting of her hopes. Springtime held so much promise for the future.

As the soggy ground dried again, Bill taught her to ride and manage a cowpony. In the evenings he wiped the dishes for her while Sis sewed on tiny nightgowns and other little garments.

Often the girls coaxed him into tuning up his guitar and singing range ballads. His shy loneliness found a sympathetic response in Carrie, and he talked to her about his work. Besides doing chores about the shack each day, he and Worden Vandervoort rode along the watercourses to drop a rope on any animals that were mired down, or to doctor cattle poisoned by eating certain plants. His brother George, Bill told her, was running a small herd of cattle on his homestead acreage, besides raising some hay and grain. Later in the spring Sis and he would plant a vegetable garden.

Spring roundup started in May, he explained, when all the outfits branded their young stock. Afterwards they drove it off winter range into country for summer grazing.

Carrie hinted wistfully that she'd love to see a roundup.

"Mebbe we can arrange it," he half promised.

"But whenever we planned to do anything together, Sis always had work for Bill to do. If Sis were invited along, though, the plans had a way of working out. Frequently, she sent him to help George at the Titus sheep ranch, as lambing and shearing seasons were the busiest periods. Did Sis think I was taking up too much of Bill's time, or was she going to become a slave-driver? The obvious explanation that Sis was jealous never occurred to me then, because it was my first experience with a love affair. But she made one strange remark that caused me to wonder. Bill had just brought in an armload of kindling for the morning fire, and when he went out to the woodpile, Sis said, 'Billy's such a nice kid, too bad he's not George's age.' " George was a little older than his wife.

"Why?" Carrie naturally asked in her innocence.

"Oh," Sis hedged, "because —," and quickly changed the subject.

When George came home to visit Sis, about once a month, Carrie and Bill had a chance to slip away for a ride. Carrie observed, however, that during these visits Sis paid more attention to Bill than to her husband. But George either didn't notice, or didn't care, although he seemed genuinely solicitous

Chapter 2 — Spring Roundup and Carrie's Betrothal

for his wife's welfare. At least, he gave no sign of feeling left out, or of being jealous of his younger brother.

"These incidents soon skipped my memory because I found many interesting things to do each day. After helping Sis bake, or wash clothes and tidy up the shack as it was called on the range, I would wander over the prairie and into ravines searching for wildflowers unfamiliar to me. I'd pick a generous handful and try to arrange a new color scheme to ornament the supper table every evening. Bill never failed to remark about my 'home decorating talents.' When he rode away to join the spring roundup crew, I continued my afternoon strolls, content to dream about him.

These long walks while Sis took a nap gave me privacy and also isolation from her frequent irritable moods. I excused Sis because of her condition. But I spent as much time apart from her as I could."

Carrie preferred the company of prairie dogs, which cheeped at her proximity to their burrows. Even ungainly jackrabbits, that startled her whenever they sprang from a sagebush cover and bounded away in long leaps, were more companionable than her snappish sister.

Solitary rambles also became a welcome sedative for her fraying nerves. Those first spring days the sun poured on the plains like warm honey, so mellow it was, softening the air to a drowsy balminess. It harmonized with the flood of emotion within her. Her thoughts constantly dwelled on Bill, how good-naturedly he accepted Sis' bossing, how he threw back his head when he sang, how easily he sat in the saddle, and how boyishly handsome he looked in a ten-gallon hat. She recalled every word of his last conversation, the tone of his voice, the gestures of hand, expressions of eye and mouth so characteristic of him. She even imagined how his kiss would feel upon her lips, and wondered when they would share the first one.

Every vagrant breeze carried a symphony of sweet scents from growing plants. Breathing deeply of their fragrances, she became lost in her dreams. Intuitively, she knew that this outpouring of feeling was the burgeoning of love. Every night she dropped off to sleep thinking about Bill, and on awakening in the morning his image filled her mind. Did similar feelings and emotions possess him, she wondered?

Drifting along in a dream world, she never bothered her head about such practical things as finding a job. Even the knowledge that failure to find work would force her return home held no immediate terrors.

Carrie gave little heed or thought to either the privations or the hardships that surrounded her. Homesteaders had little except freedom to recommend their way of life. There were none of the comforts and few of the pleasures of living in a city. Plumbing in the kitchen or a bathroom, electric lights, telephones, and the neighborhood grocery store were nonexistent. Even to get mail most of them had to ride ten, twenty, or thirty miles to a post office. Frequently, neighbors lived that distance from one another. But Carrie gladly traded old luxuries for her new-found freedom and first love.

One sunny day in late May while Sis was sweeping the floor and Carrie was making the bed, Bill rode up to the the shack. They heard his spurs jingling before his tall, slender form blotted the doorway. Dust streaked his pants and blue shirt and covered his hat in a gray film.

He greeted them impartially, and walking toward Sis, asked if she'd like to visit the roundup today. "We're workin' on upper O'Fallon Crick. I thought you girls might like to look on."

He's tactful, Carrie thought, and noted that Sis appeared pleased because the invitation had been addressed to her.

"Oh, that'll be fun." Sis leaned on the broom, promising to ride over in the afternoon.

"Ole Monty, the cook, said he'd be countin' on yuh for chuck tonight." Bill's eyes flickered briefly at Carrie. He gave her an odd, questioning grin, but didn't tell her then that all the boys were anxious to size up the Eastern pilgrim.

"Well, see yuh later." He waved his hat and strode out.

Visiting the roundup was *the* treat which Carrie had eagerly

Chapter 2 — Spring Roundup and Carrie's Betrothal

looked forward to for a long time. The prospect of recreation put both girls in a merry mood. They chatted gaily over the morning's housework, had a light lunch, and then quickly changed from gingham dresses into long riding skirts and white shirtwaists. Carrie wore an old felt hat of George's, but Sis put on a Stetson with a flourish and rather unnecessarily flaunted it, Carrie thought. Both knotted red bandanas about their necks. Sis went striding out to the pasture and caught up Chris and Seal, the black horses of all-purpose work. Bill had taught Carrie the proper procedure of saddling, so she drew up the cinch on faithful old Seal, then climbed into the saddle borrowed from Worden Vandervoort's mother.

"Are you sure riding won't hurt you?" she anxiously asked her sister, noting the swelling of her waistline as they started off at a walk across the pasture. Sunshine spilled hotly on them out of the blue sky.

"Oh, no," Sis tossed her head airily. "I'm not that far along yet." Later on she said, "We'll get Billy to sing tonight after supper." Carrie noticed Sis' face light up at the prospect. Becoming aware of Carrie's puzzled expression, Sis called attention to the fast-growing grass. In the swale they were riding through, the blades of grama-grass reached their horses' knees.

Carrie made no reply and soon forgot the incident in the enjoyment of the ride over rolling green hills seamed by cutbanks of coulees. Several red blooms on prickly pear cactus and the white blossoms of a Maricopa lily caught her eye. Their course led past a prairie dog town. While they were skirting it the rodents sat erect on mounds near their burrows with paws folded neatly over their stomachs. At each sharp, squeaky bark the dogs jerked furry tails against their backs. Amused, Carrie watched them.

The girls located the roundup by the clouds of dust dissolving in the clear air. The camp lay below in a shallow, grass-covered valley between low hills. Fascinated, Carrie gazed at a large herd of brown and white cattle held bunched up by cowboys. The animals were in the lower end of a big field near a stream with steep cutbanks. As the girls passed through a gate in the barbed wire fence and rode down the slope, Carrie noticed a horse herd between two wagons. Sis told her that was the cavvy ponies for use when the ones they were riding played out.

In a pole corral close to a bunch of calves, Carrie could see the forms of men moving about a small fire. Since the work was a novelty to her, the girls sat their horses to watch the punchers ride in among the cattle to cut out the calves and unbranded yearlings. Amid the shouts of the men the cows bawled for their offspring, which were being dragged on the end of a rope into the square corral for branding.

Suddenly, Carrie caught sight of Bill on his cutting-out horse, a clean-limbed iron gray. He was galloping alongside the calf herd, heading off a fractious cow that tried to break into it. Twirling a lariat over his head, he sent the loop flying toward the cow. By good luck rather than skill it settled over her horns. The horse slid back on his haunches, jerking the cow off her feet and holding the rope taut so she couldn't get up. Carrie thought the intelligence of the cowponies, trained to their work as thoroughly as their riders, was truly remarkable. In a few seconds Bill urged his horse to slacken the rope. Chastened, the cow rose heavily to her feet and in a docile manner trotted back to the herd.

"Hey, Billy!" Sis shouted.

He paused in coiling his rope to glance up and wave to the girls, then finished his task and rode back to his work.

"Why doesn't he come over to say hello?" Carrie asked, hurt by what she considered Bill's yokel rudeness.

"He's too bashful before the other punchers."

Carrie fixed her attention on the other cowboys. Most were nice-looking, smooth-shaven, lanky young men in their twenties who sat loosely erect in their saddles. They didn't dress according to her preconceived ideas, formed by reading Western romances. Only three or four out of the twenty she counted wore leather chaps. But all had on work pants, black boots, and hickory or light cotton shirts. The men riding in and out of the dusty herd had knotted their bandana handkerchiefs over nose and mouth. Without exception all wore unbuttoned vests and high-crowned Stetson hats.

Occasionally a cowboy rode past the girls on a sweaty, dust-caked horse and gave them a curious stare. Each rider made for the cavvy held in a triangular-shaped corral, improvised by stretching ropes between the wheels of the chuck and bed wagons. Unsaddling the tired mount, he turned the animal inside, then walked along the outside of the corral, a lariat loop dangling from his right hand. When he located the fresh pony he wanted, he flipped the noose over its head and led it out to be saddled.

Carrie suggested they ride over closer to the cavvy. Her eyes opened wider than usual as they approached the horse herd and she gave a low whistle, estimating there must be "a hundred and fifty horses in there!" Some animals were moving restlessly about; others stood and gazed in curiosity at the girls. Still others were cropping the flattened grass.

Sis explained that each "cowpoke" had seven to nine ponies in his string.

The variety of colors impressed Carrie, as she had never known there were so many. Although bays predominated, she picked out what Sis said were roans, buckskins, blacks, grays, chestnuts or "sorrels" and pintos.

"They don't use any mares on the roundup," Sis was explaining when a man's voice behind them interrupted.

He asked "Miz Elsie" if her friend would like to see the "brandin"?

Sis twisted in the saddle. "Oh, hello, Monty." She introduced Carrie to the cook, a grizzled, elderly man with merry blue eyes and one leg shorter than the other.

Sis grinned teasingly at her tenderfoot sister as she told Monty that Carrie didn't want to miss anything — " 'specially any good-lookin' punchers."

Carrie flushed and stammered, "How you do spread it on!" Turning to Monty, she said she'd enjoy watching them brand. . . . They had just seen Bill lasso a cow.

Monty reckoned Bill "was plumb busy," making an apology for that young man's neglect. "They're tryin' to git all the young stuff branded today, so's to begin dippin' tomorrer."

"Dipping?" Carrie cautiously inquired, suspecting one of the tall tales always perpetrated on gullible tenderfeet like the mythical Double Diamond D-Bar Dot Ranch.

Monty told her in a serious tone, "Cattle gotta be dipped in creosote vats to kill ticks an' prevent disease spreadin'. If yuh like, I'll stake out yore hosses, then show yuh around."

Carrie thanked him and dismounted.

Monty was an old buckaroo, Sis remarked, dismounting also. He knew the cow business inside out.

"But I got all busted up breakin' outlaws," he explained. "Cain't ride much no more."

In the obliging way of the Westerner he removed the bridles, loosened the cinches, and tied their horses to picket ropes. They immediately started grazing. Until time to prepare supper, he chatted with the girls and patiently made sensible explanations to Carrie's host of questions. Finally excusing himself, he limped away to the chuckwagon. Sis joked with nearly every man in the crew. She seemed to know them all.

When Monty's cheery call to "Come an' git it!" rang out, the girls were at the branding corral where the foreman, sitting atop the fence, kept tally with a lead pencil in a vest-sized notebook. He listed the number of bull and heifer calves belonging to his own and other outfits.

Even the acrid smell of burned hair, smoke, and dust failed to spoil Carrie's appetite when she sniffed the fragrant, blended odors of sourdough biscuits and steaks cooking in the Dutch oven, and the aroma of freshly ground coffee boiling. Monty had let down the end-gate of the chuckwagon. From this platform table the girls helped themselves to a tin plate and cup off the stack and to a knife, fork, and spoon from a large pan. Monty, squatted by the fire, served them a fried steak, a potato boiled with the jacket on, and a ladle full of boiled beans. Then

Chapter 2 — Spring Roundup and Carrie's Betrothal

he motioned them to a pan of brown gravy that rested on glowing coals under the pot-rack.

By ones and twos the cowboys drifted in, helped themselves, and found a place to sit on their heels with the tin dish balanced on their knees. The cup of coffee they set on the ground beside them. Bill and Worden Vandervoort came together and joined Carrie and Sis who were sitting cross-legged on the grass, their long riding skirts tucked under them. The meal was a silent affair, the men too hungry and fatigued to converse. The sun had slid toward the rim of the prairie, throwing long shadows on the camp scene.

Once Bill said, "Like it?" and Carrie answered him loud enough for Monty, over by the fire, to hear, that every moment had thrilled her. She'd never forget this day, nor the wonderful food. These were the most delicious sourdough biscuits she had ever tasted.

She was about to take her third three-inch thick one, baked a perfect golden brown, when Monty, a pleased grin on his face, called to her, "Wait, Miss Carrie, I want yuh to save room for my gingerbread and stewed blackberries. I made a special hot sauce for it when Bill told me you girls was comin'." He served her a helping big enough to throw one of the roundup crew. Carrie didn't have the heart to leave any of it, although her waistline was becoming uncomfortably tight.

At last, stuffed, she lolled backward in groaning contentment. Bill took her dishes and then fetched his bedroll, propping it as a back rest for her and Sis. He excused himself with a laconic, "Be seein' yuh," and walked over to the bedwagon.

Idly, Carrie watched the men as they finished supper carry their empty dishes to the chuckwagon and drop them into a deep basin. Some pulled sacks of Bull Durham tobacco from their vest pockets and rolled cigarettes with one hand; others lighted up and smoked a curved stem pipe. Bill, she noticed, had taken his shaving things from his war bag, stropped his razor on the inside of his boot, and shaved by a hand mirror hung from the endgate rod of the bedwagon. She smiled to herself, for his beard at eighteen was not much more than a fuzzy down. The cook and the night wrangler were drying dishes, while another man busied himself chopping wood. The foreman walked up to the cook and day wrangler and told them where to make the next day's camp at noon and at night.

Worden, who had been talking to Sis, produced a harmonica, slapped it on his hand to jar out dust and dirt, and began playing the lilting melody of "The Old Chisholm Trail." On the other side of her, Carrie heard a group of men arguing whether Teddy Roosevelt would get elected president on the Bull Moose ticket. Another pair were discussing the sinking of the *Titanic*. Most "allowed they'd ruther fork the hurricane deck of a bronc than ride in one of them newfangled boats."

Sparks rose from the campfire that flickered a bright orange in the deepening twilight. The air had cooled and stars began to glimmer in the pale turquoise evening sky. Hearing a movement beside her, Carrie glanced up and saw Bill. He leaned over to whisper while Sis was singing and looking the other way, "Wanta come along while I water Chief?" He had put on a clean white shirt.

They sauntered away from the lounging forms of the men over to his saddled gray, tied by a rope to the wheel of the bed-wagon. The bridle hung from the horn and the cinch was loose, she noticed. Leading Chief, the two walked down the slope to a gravel bar on the creek's bank. Straggling clumps of willows, a few cottonwoods and ash saplings grew along the margin. The pony blew dust from his nose before thrusting it into the clear water. Over low hills in the east the moon was just rising and the night breeze carried the muted strains of the "Cowboy's Lament," played on the harmonica and a zither harp. The fresh scent of mint and marsh grasses floated on the damp air.

Bill squatted down to dip a drink in the rolled brim of his hat. His silent, preoccupied manner puzzled Carrie. Rising, he placed the sombrero on the back of his head and began deliberately but clumsily to "build a smoke."

In a low, constrained voice, pitched scarcely above the

Chapter 2 — Spring Roundup and Carrie's Betrothal

purling of the stream, he complained it seemed like he never got a chance to "see yuh alone," and there was a heap of things he'd like "to trade talk about."

Carrie pointed out they were alone now, while thinking how quickly he had picked up cowboy idiom. She didn't think Sis had noticed their absence.

He struck a match on his thumbnail and held it in cupped hands to his cigarette. In its flare she saw that his hands shook and that he took a deep breath before he plunged on. Possibly the darkness helped to loosen his shy reserve.

He said he "figgered on takin' up a homestead of his own, and runnin' a few cattle mebbe. If she'd like to settle down out here, too, well, he thought —." He paused to take another long draw on his cigarette, then started over as smoke drifted out his nostrils.

He guessed she knew how he felt about her by now. He was not "bridle-wise how to say it, but gee, Carrie, you kin plumb git me throwed, hogtied, and earmarked — not right away," he added hastily, but when she'd a mind to. Leaning against the saddle he peered anxiously at her in the dusk. He just thought he'd mention it now, he went on diffidently, and she could think it over and tell him her answer later.

Her pulses leaped frantically, and she felt all choked up inside — pride, happiness, love struggled for dominance. She knew he was asking, in rangeland idiom, to marry her. Even in the midst of exquisite excitement, she realized she must keep her head. Outside of roundup work, Bill didn't have a paying job, nor a thin dime.

She tried to control her voice from too deeply showing her emotions as she said, "I'm glad to give you my promise — now. But we can't be married soon. Things are going to be pretty hard for Sis from now on. Besides, I'd like to teach a year to get a little money ahead — for our home. Maybe — well — maybe we oughtn't to plan on getting married until sometime next year."

"Well, if that's the way yuh feel about it — but you'll give me your word?" he insisted, and reached forward bashfully to take her into his arms.

His strong, young embrace, the warmth of his lips, the cleanshaven scent of him, mingled with tobacco, caused tingles along her spine. Trembling shook him, whether from nervous excitement or the ardor of his affection, she was uncertain.

They heard Sis calling. Chief lifted his head, ears perked, water dripping from his muzzle.

"Yes, Bill," she whispered against his lips. Abruptly he released her with a muttered, "Damn."

Carrie called to Sis' approaching form that they were coming as she stepped away from Bill.

"What're you kids doing?" Sis demanded from the top of the cutbank, and staring at them on the creek's edge, reminded "Billy" all the boys had been wanting him to sing. "Come on now, and do your stuff."

Carrie said quickly, "Please do," to mollify Sis.

"Aw, shucks." Bill's tone revealed a wealth of disappointment and vexation, but in silent obedience and leading the gray he followed Carrie up the path.

Later in the evening on the ride back to the homestead, while the moon was shining full and stars winked brightly, scarcely a word was spoken. Bill had insisted on accompanying the girls, and two other cowboys volunteered to go "for the ride." Carrie sensed a sullen tension in Sis, and Bill had withdrawn into his shell of reserve. Even the punchers lapsed into a silent mood, although they had been making sheep's-eyes at Carrie during the impromptu musicale.

After the boys bade them goodnight at the corral, Sis had little to say. The girls went on to the house and began undressing by lamplight. Carried guessed that Sis must have noticed a glow in her eyes, for she brusquely asked, "Did Billy kiss you tonight?"

Something defiant in Carrie prompted her to retort, "Yes, we got engaged."

"It's ridiculous, he's nothing but a kid. He can't support you."

"We won't be married before next year. Probably in June." That seemed to pacify Sis. So *much* could happen in twelve months!

Chapter 3

Episodes on a Sheep Ranch 1912

Summer's advance turned the green range to a tawny tan. Carrie loved the rolling expanse of the plains, the clay cutbanks along streams carved out by high-water freshets in the spring, and the draws or coulees that sheltered cottonwood trees and scrub pines. Even fierce rain and hail squalls, the plague of horseflies and buffalo gnats, or "noseeums" as the Indians called them, failed to quench her ardor for the new freedom she found in the cattle country. At first the red scoria (cindered lava) hills on the badlands' edge seemed ugly and dreary, but in time she grew accustomed to their fantastic shapes and considered them picturesque. Salt sage, greasewood, prickly pear cactus, Spanish bayonet, and grama-grass that everywhere sprinkled the prairie took on a friendly, commonplace appearance, as did the willows and cottonwoods clustered along creek banks.

"But things were not going well with Sis and George. It had been a hard year and they would have no beef cattle to sell after the fall roundup. In fact, Sis confided to me that they would find themselves broke before summer had passed, so she hired out to 'Old High-Pockets' Titus, owner of the sheep ranch where

George was working.* She arranged for Bill to look after things at the homestead.

"I offered to share the housekeeping chores since 'Old High-Pockets' was a widower. Sis accepted with alacrity. We girls packed a suitcase apiece and Bill drove us in the wagon to the Titus place toward Ismay. Sunlight cast long shadows over the largest spread I had yet seen. The ranch buildings occupied a grassy, wooded flat alongside a flowing stream. The house had a yard fenced off from corrals, wagon shed, and barn. Poplar trees grew around the wire fence, giving the whole place a long lived-in, well-ordered, prosperous appearance."

Carrie commented it was more like a town house, thinking of the homesteaders' tarpaper stacks.

He'd been established a good many years, Sis told her, "got in on the free range."

Carrie asked why they called him "High-Pockets."

"Wait'll you see him." Sis' eyes crinkled at her sister, and Bill grinned in secretly shared amusement.

Shepherd dogs ran out barking noisily as the team rattled up the lane toward the kitchen door. When High-Pockets' lank six feet, four inches, came striding in a loose-jointed way down the back porch steps, Carrie decided the name aptly described his long-shanked legs and short waist. This tagging of nicknames on those having pronounced characteristics, mental or physical, was a custom peculiar to the cattle country, she had observed. Oddly, the cowboys only dubbed the people they liked. Several months after her arrival, she learned that a certain prim Victorianism in her nature had earned her the sobriquet of "Touch-me-not."

"Old High-Pockets had a wide grin," she recalled, "that literally seemed stretched from ear to ear, displaying tobacco-stained teeth. He held out his hand in genuine cordiality to Bill and Sis. I noted his gray hair, long nose, grizzled beard, and prominent Adam's apple."

---

* *"High-Pockets" was possibly O. W. Titus of Ismay who ran 2,500 head of sheep, according to a local news item in the Miles City* **American** *in 1915.*

Chapter 3 — Episodes on a Sheep Ranch

With a courtliness at odds with his social status and appearance, he helped Carrie out of the wagon. Upon being introduced, he stared down into her comely face with its regular features, wide-open eyes below heavy, quizzically arched eyebrows, framed by black, wavy hair beneath an old felt hat.

In a mild, teasing voice he exclaimed, "My, my, but I'll git a lot of work done this summer, 'cause all the young bucks'll want to hang around the ranch to be near you." He laughed softly at his own joke.

Carrie blushed at the compliment, which brought a frown to Bill's tanned face.

Later, when sheepherders came to the kitchen every evening on one excuse or another and loafed, High-Pockets complained to Sis, "Dog gone, I can't git the boys to do no work I pay for, 'cause they all want to hang around to see if Touch-me-not is goin' to wash dishes."

Surrounded by admiring swains, the thought frequently passed through Carrie's mind, if her father could only see her now! Thought of him and her unhappy home life strengthened her determination to get a job teaching, so she wouldn't be forced to return to Wisconsin. Career opportunities for women in the rangeland were extremely limited in 1912. Of the two professions — teaching or nursing — the former appealed most because it would enable Carrie to live in the country. A shadow of doubt crossed her mind every time she thought about jobs, for summer was passing. Although she had made inquiries, her search had been fruitless. She did learn that she would have to take the State Teacher's Examinations. If she passed, there was a chance. If she didn't, she decided to stay on with High-Pockets as housekeeper.

Bill was away much of the time on the roundup and keeping an eye on George's homestead, but Carrie had very little leisure to be lonesome. She kept busy helping Sis with the endless treadmill of household drudgery — cooking and baking, washing dishes, scrubbing floors, dusting, sewing and ironing. Before meals she ground the fresh coffee beans. By July chokecherries and tart buffaloberries growing abundantly in pasture thickets had ripened, so the girls spent alternate afternoons picking and making them into jelly and jam. As long as the season lasted, they gathered the luscious serviceberries for dessert.

In addition, there were orphan, injured, or sick lambs requiring special care. Lambing time had begun in May, followed by the shearing of the mature animals' fleece about mid-June. Those were busy months on a sheep ranch. A part of most evenings Carrie spent brushing up on arithmetic, history, English, geography, and other studies prescribed as subjects for grammar schools by the State Board of Education.

One hot afternoon Carrie, wearing a freshly starched gingham apron, was drying dishes and humming the tune of "Red River Valley." She was thinking about Bill and about making a batch of cookies. Sis was resting on the sofa in the front room. The drain pan sat on the kitchen table near the open windows overlooking the barn and corrals. Flies buzzed in the close, still air. From brush in the creek bottom a bird warbled merry notes intermittently. Now and then a young rooster flapped his wings and crowed a lusty squeak in challenge. Absorbed in her thoughts, she paid no attention to the drumming hooves of a horse, nor to the approach of clinking spurs, until the screen door behind her creaked open. She turned to see Bill's tall form standing in the doorway. His hickory shirt clung in dark blue damp patches to his broad chest. Dust filled the creases of his overalls and black riding boots.

"Howdy," he greeted her, grinning diffidently.

Carrie gasped in surprise and pleasure, asking if the roundup was over so soon.

Before answering, he took off his dusty Stetson and wiped the sweat from his forehead on his shirtsleeve. His chestnut-brown hair lay in damp strands on top.

"N-no. Jist thought I'd drift over to see how things are goin' with you. It's been a long time since I seen yuh."

Tossing his hat on the stable, he made for the dipper in the granite pail. While swallowing the cool water in thirsty gulps his brown eyes scrutinized Carrie who was still drying plates.

"Any them sheepherders been hangin' 'round yuh lately?"

Shaking her head, she smiled reassuringly at him. So, jealousy of the ranch hands had impelled him to make the ride in the heat.

He got to thinking, he explained, that some of them "might have plumb overstepped their reach with *my* girl." Later on he admitted that fear of losing her had haunted him night and day and finally panicked him. Casting reason to the winds, he had ridden in desperate haste to reassure himself that she still cared for him. Now that he was here, he had become tongue-tied, and was too bashful to even take her in his arms and kiss her. Everything seemed so matter-of-fact. How could he explain his fears about her? They would sound too silly.

Carrie noted how ill-at-ease he acted, like a small boy caught with cookies bulging his pants pockets. Giving him a sidelong glance as she stacked the plates, she asked if he was riding close to the homestead now.

He hung up the dipper and wiped his mouth on back of his hand. "Well," he admitted reluctantly, "we're workin' toward the badlands, but it's only forty miles away —"

"Forty miles!" Carrie exclaimed, aghast. "Why, Bill, you'd better hustle right back there before the crew misses you." Bill had ridden forty miles and risked his job just to see her — his fiancée, as she reminded herself many times a day. His devotion deeply touched her.

Meekly, he agreed.

Hearing their voices, Sis came into the kitchen and said with some asperity, "You'll get canned, Billy, if the boss gets wind of this. Foolin' 'round Carrie when you ought to be on the job won't get you nowhere."

Bill flushed and picked up his ten-gallon hat. He nervously fingered the brim. "Well, I'll be hittin' the trail. . . . See yuh later," he threw at Carrie as he clumped out, spurs clinking dully from hard boot thumps.

A hot and cold wave of anger spread through Carrie. She banged the plate down on the cupboard shelf, then whirled toward Sis, demanding through clenched teeth, "Why did you have to say that?"

Taken by surprise, Sis started, but instantly recovered. "D'you want the kid to lose his job?" she countered evenly.

For seconds Carrie glared at Sis, acutely conscious of her misshapen figure partly concealed by an old wrapper, of her braided hair hanging down her back. Irritation and resentment at her sister's interference finally gave way to her old bashful reserve. Sharp words of rebuke on her tongue were not spoken then. After all she couldn't risk upsetting Sis too much. Probably her condition explained her attitude anyhow.

Carrie shrugged and said in a resigned tone that this wasn't getting the dishes done.

Without speaking Sis turned and left the room. The thought comforted Carrie that if she could only get a job teaching, it would separate her from Sis and all the unpleasantness she must endure until the baby came. Thinking it over later, she wished she had forced matters to a showdown.

Some time after the incident, High-Pockets drove Carrie to a siding where she caught the train to Miles City. In high anticipation she took the teachers' examinations for which she had been preparing all summer. Just before leaving the ranch she had told Sis if she got a job she'd send Sis half her salary — for the baby.

"You'll do no such thing," Sis emphatically declined. "I won't have it! You're welcome to share my last crust, an' you know it."

Her sister was certainly an odd contradiction, Carrie reflected, and forgave all her faults because of her generosity.

Carrie's parents had been urging her to return home and get ready to enter the state university in the fall. But a job would give her the perfect excuse to remain in the West until her marriage. Although she and Bill had made no public announcement of their engagement, she had written the news to her mother, asking it be withheld from her father. Her mother hoped that William was "a nice, steady, young man," and that she would be very happy.

Back at High-Pockets' ranch, Carrie impatiently awaited word from the school board. Had she passed the exams? Would she be offered a teaching position? For the first time since coming West, her mind was filled with other thoughts than those of her sweetheart.

Several weeks went by and she became prey to gloomy doubts. Then one rainy morning in September she was alone in the kitchen doing the week's baking. Sis was making the beds. High-Pockets, George, and the other men were down at the toolshed. While kneading the dough Carrie was keenly aware of the monotonous dripping of water off the eaves, her ear keyed up for the sound of Bill's step. He had ridden to Ismay's general store and post office for the mail. The spring roundup was over and the fall beef roundup hadn't started yet, so Bill divided his time between the homestead and High-Pockets' ranch. Time dragged on his hands in rainy weather, unless he was doing something.

Just as she placed the last pan of bread into the warming oven to rise, he opened the door, bringing an aura of wet, cool air into the hot room. She closed the oven quickly and turned to gaze questioningly at him.

"Here's that letter yuh been all steamed up about."

He handed her a long, thick envelope, bearing the return address of the Custer County Board of Education, Courthouse Building, Miles City. Eagerly, with trembling fingers, she tore a strip off one end and pulled out a crisp sheet of paper and a printed contract. While she skimmed the contents, Bill hung up his slicker, then perched on the table's edge to watch.

"I kin hardly wait," he dubiously prompted at last. "Did yuh, or didn't yuh?"

"It's from the county superintendent," she replied in a tremulous voice. "I passed all right. This is a notice the North Sunday Creek school has a vacancy. Course, it doesn't pay very much, and there's only seven children in the district, but it's a job! Oh, Bill, aren't you glad?" Clutching paper and contract in her hands she danced across the floor, threw her arms about his neck and hugged him. "Whatever I can save will be for us! For our homestead."

"Whoa! Whoa, there!" Taken by surprise at her display of affection, he recovered quickly and, encouraged, kissed her. Shy kisses they were and wet from the rain. Then he held her at arm's length. "Gee, the little schoolma'am. She's got flour on her nose." He gently brushed it off, then suddenly demanded, "Where's this Sunday Crick school at?"

"It's northwest of Miles."

Disappointment clouded his brown eyes. "Aw, gee, then we can't see each other all winter."

She patted his tanned, rain-wet cheek and tried to reassure him it was only from October to May — eight months — and she'd write him every day and mail him a weekly letter.

"I wish yuh wouldn't go so far away. I don't like the way things been stackin' up," he said.

"It's only about eighty miles. Promise to write me?"

"Shore as shootin'. But your leavin' makes me plumb skittish as a bronc."

"Don't you trust me?" Carrie gazed intently into his eyes.

"It isn't that." He looked off into the distance, seeming at a loss how to put his fears into words.

"Then, if you trust me, what's there to be afraid of?"

"Well, it's jist a feelin', I guess." He sighed, then grinned suddenly, his face boyishly lighting up. Pulling her to him, he kissed her possessively several times, until they heard Sis' footsteps approaching. With a scowl he let go of her and hastily began rolling a cigarette.

The first week in October when she said goodbye to everyone at the Titus ranch, Sis seemed relieved, Carrie thought, but whether at getting rid of her or keeping her away from Bill, Carrie was uncertain. She left a few days earlier than necessity required. Perhaps Sis was getting as tired of her as she was of her sister. But she didn't care. Her great chance had come. The signing of the contract marked the declaration of her economic independence from her father. At last she would be a wage-earner. Happy pride filled her. Her only regret was being separated from Bill. This drive to the station with him would be the last time she would see him for months, or at least until the Christmas holidays.

Chapter 4

Trials and Tribulations of a Country Schoolma'am 1912-1913

Upon arrival in Miles City, Carrie reported to the board of education. The secretary informed her that Mrs. Denny M. Smith, who had arranged to board and room the teacher, would come to the hotel to take her to the Smith place near the school. It was Carrie's first leisured opportunity to look over the town of one- and two-story brick and frame buildings, located near the east bank of Tongue River where it emptied into the Yellowstone. On the west a grove of cottonwood trees bordered the city limits, and about three miles beyond on the river's west bank was the cavalry garrison of Fort Keogh.

The hotel's day clerk, a stubby-whiskered "old-timer" as he styled himself, who had broken his leg "tryin' to curry the kinks outa a bronc's backbone," told Carrie that Miles was a feverish cowtown during stock shipping time. He urged her to be on hand in April when the Stockgrowers' Association held its annual convention and the streets were gaily decorated with bunting and banners.

Finding her a willing listener, he reminisced on the old days, describing the wood-burning, paddle-wheel steamers that used to haul supplies for the post up the Yellowstone from Dakota Territory. He yarned by the hour about fights between the Sioux Indians and soldiers, and claimed to have visited the Custer battlefield "right after the fightin' quit." When she admitted being the new teacher for "the first school on North Sunday Creek," it reminded him that herds on the old Texas or Northern trail used to "go up that there crick's west side on the way to the Musselshell River. That's where Con Kohrs and other big cattle fellers first stocked the ranges in Judith Basin. Them days was the beginnin' of the cattle business in this here state."

He helped to pass the time by describing the country's colorful frontier past — the days of buffalo hunters, the bull-whackers' freight wagons, steamboats, Indian scouts, and free grass range. It was the "honyockers" (homesteaders), he declared, who put most big cattle outfits out of business by putting up barbed wire fences and plowing grassland to farm. Some old brands he mentioned were the Hat X on Timber "Crick" near the Little Dry, the CK, and the XIT (Ten-in-Texas) near the Hat ranch where Bob Fudge from Texas was once foreman. Those three spreads used to hold roundups in common and all were north of "Milestown" (its former name). Closer to Carrie's school was the Bow and Arrow ranch (locally called the Bow Gun) on South Sunday Creek. Again a feeling of new adventures about to begin aroused her expectations and excitement on arrival in the rangeland.

On the day appointed for her to leave, an Indian summer afternoon with a blue haze lying on sun-washed, low hills outside town, Carrie waited in an old leather chair in the lobby, suitcases beside her. Flies buzzed about the windows. Old-timer lounged in the next chair, recounting the time Teddy Roosevelt had visited the Stockgrowers' Convention, and punctuating his recital by skillfully directing jets of tobacco juice into a tall, brass cuspidor. The pungent, rank odor of it assailed her nostrils, almost nauseating her.

A few cattlemen in dark business suits, high-heeled boots,

Chapter 4 — Trials and Tribulations of a Country Schoolma'am

and sombreros, who stared in friendly curiosity at her, came and went. The thumping of their boots on the linoleum floor briefly disturbed the quiet. An occasional rig or horseback rider passed along the street and stirred up puffs of dust. Several troopers from Keogh swaggered past the windows. One of them espied her and winked. Idly, she watched a skinny team hitched to a dilapidated buckboard rattle up to the tie-rail before the hotel. A little old man with a gray mustache got out, and coming into the lobby announced to the clerk that he had "come to git the schoolmarm. Missus Smith couldn't make it." His striped shirt with soft collar was innocent of a tie, and his black suit was both spotted and wrinkled. Carrie mentally catalogued him as one of the hired hands.

"This here's Mr. Petrie," the clerk introduced him.

Carrie bade Old-timer goodbye and followed George E. "Old Man" Petrie, as he was usually called, out to the rig. He flung the suitcases in the rear, then clambered in and turned the front wheels so that she could climb in easier. In silence he started the team by slapping the lines on their backs. They turned a corner, and soon they crossed the Yellowstone River and headed northwest.

One native Montanan, Margaret Mann, who grew up at Fort Keogh, described that sparsely settled, undeveloped countryside from her childhood memory in a letter to the writer (July 7, 1982): "The south side of the Yellowstone River was much more settled than the north side. South side land was more fertile, there was plenty of water. Ranchers were closer together and possibly more prosperous. The north side of the river consisted of two counties, Custer and Dawson, and they covered almost half of Montana. There were only five other counties in the state and I remember learning the names of them all when I was in school — no great job for only seven. Custer County north of the Yellowstone River and Dawson County were unsurveyed and you could locate any place you could find water for yourself and stock, or hide out from the law."

Carrie recalled: "The horses went plod, plod, plod for mile

Carrie Cather, the homesteader's sister who became a country schoolteacher and rancher's wife. (Courtesy, President Lydia Fleming and Executive Board, Range Rider Reps, from *Fanning the Embers,* Miles City.)

after mile, following two wheel tracks winding through dry prairie grass among clumps of sage. A few wire fences had caught the dried tumbleweeds of Russian thistle. An owl sat boldly on a post. Its large, yellow eyes stared unblinkingly at us. A ditch of muddy water lay beside the road's course for some distance, drainage from the fall rains, I supposed. Two hawks were lazily soaring high against the sky, alternately flapping their wings and gliding, probably in search of a cow carcass or other carrion."

While observing the scenery, Carrie speculated what her new boardinghouse would be like. A tarpaper homesteader's shack, perhaps, like the Vandervoorts' — or a prosperous ranch house?

Chapter 4 — Trials and Tribulations of a Country Schoolma'am

Well, no matter. She'd soon find out. The important thing was her great adventure and first real job. She anticipated the immediate future with the high hopes and inexperience of an eighteen-year-old. Her curiosity was even further stimulated because unpleasant relations with Sis had just ended.

Descending a hilly slope, they drove through a region overgrown by prickly pear cactus, Spanish bayonet, and low sagebrush. Beyond the valley of North Sunday Creek eastward were red buttes of scoria. In a broken country of coulees and canyons they added colorful and fantastic features to the landscape. It was the longest trip Carrie ever made, it seemed, because her companion, unlike the clerk, was not talkative.

"What odd hills," she finally remarked to encourage conversation. Bare of vegetation, their reddish-brown, gravelly slopes were seamed by gullies.

Old Man Petrie made a rasping sound in his throat, and volunteered, "Homesteaders call 'em the 'devil's ash heaps.' "

Carrie smiled. "How interesting!"

Instead of becoming chatty, her companion pulled a quid of tobacco from his hip pocket and, biting off a generous hunk, began to chew industriously. From then on, aside from an occasional comment as to whether she was pretty tired, or that "it wa'n't very fur — only ten mile — and arter you've made the trip a few times it wunt seem fur," his conversational efforts struck the doldrums.

The road began winding upward around pointed buttes and over ridges topped with scrub cedar and jack-pine to emerge on a rolling, grassy plateau or tableland. Here and there masses of colored rocks, mostly brick-red, stood out among wind and sun-cured buffalo grass and blue joint. The range now looked brown and parched. Although it was a region exposed to the hot sun and wind, driving hail, swarms of insects, and might be considered desolate by some, it held a fascination for her. She would never exchange the clean smell of sage and the rangeland's vastness for all the green meadows and wooded hills on her father's farm.

Toward late afternoon they turned off onto a side road. The horses headed, of their own accord, into a homestead where a group of unpainted, board buildings scarred the prairie landscape by their ugliness. Chickens, geese, and a pig or two wandered about the yard, and a rooster stood with impudent familiarity in the kitchen doorway. A shaggy bird dog trotted up to greet him, wagging tail and rear quarters in the way that setters do. Old Man Petrie pulled up the tired nags. A wave of repulsion and sickening disappointment swept through Carrie.

"I wanted to scream, to cry, to run away and hide in the cleanness of the plains. But I was too timid to show my feelings, so I only sat in the buggy and stared.

"From a lean-to attached to the house out waddled a fat woman, weighing a generous three-hundred pounds on the foot, it seemed to me. She wasn't more than five feet tall and looked like an animated apple dumpling. Giving me one indifferent glance, she waddled back into the shed. I gasped, unprepared for such a snubbing in this country of warm-hearted hospitality."

"Oh, Babe," Petrie called, "c'mon out here an' meet the new schoolmarm." Turning to Carrie, he explained, "That's my darter, Missus Smith."

"The said daughter again emerged and gave me a quick jerk of the head which passed for a sociable acknowledgement of the introduction. Her face, I observed this time, was mostly tiers of chins. Long strands of brown hair straggled about her face from two braids hanging down her back. The hair's weight upon her head, she explained later, gave her a headache. A dirty, torn apron covered her shapeless bulk. But piercing blue eyes swept me from head to foot as the 'new schoolmarm' got out of the buckboard. Then she turned without a word and entered the house."

Old Man Petrie apologized for his daughter's rudeness, saying, "She's busy churnin'." He told Carrie to "g'wan in the shed, and she'll show you around when she gits through."

Carrie lifted long skirts to pick her way gingerly through

Chapter 4 — *Trials and Tribulations of a Country Schoolma'am*

chickens and geese that indignantly hissed at her, and stooped to enter the lean-to. Two little tow-headed girls, about six or eight, stood near a woodpile turning the handle on a wooden churn. They smiled shyly as she watched them with friendly interest.

"What's your name?" she asked the older of the two. They would be her pupils, she guessed.

In a low voice the taller girl answered, "Minnie."

Looking at the younger one, Carrie prompted, "And your name is?" But the smaller child lowered her head and shuffled a bare toe in the dust. "Come on, little one," she pressed, "you're not afraid to tell me your name, are you?" As the little girl went on squirming, Carrie said in a teasing way, "What's happened to your tongue? Did the cat steal it?"

Because her sister still refused to answer, Minnie volunteered, "She's Maria."

The two girls continued churning in silence, occasionally darting side-glances at Carrie. When they finished they laid the cover on the churn, but failed to clamp it. Maria, in her embarrassment, bumped it and tipped it over. Some of the butter spilled out and rolled on the ground under the geese roost.

Just then Mrs. Smith waddled in and, seeing the mishap, sprayed the air with profane language.

"It was an accident!" Carrie protested. "They didn't mean to —."

Ignoring her, Mrs. Smith got down heavily on her knees, scooped up the butter, rinsed it briefly in a bucket of water and put it back in the churn.

"It's gotta go to town in the mornin'," she growled.

A queasy feeling gripped Carrie's stomach. How could she ever relish a meal cooked by Mrs. Smith?

Fastening the clamp on the churn, Mrs. Smith turned to Carrie and said in a more amiable tone, "C'mon in and set a spell. Ye must be tired after that long drive with Pa."

Carrie followed her with misgivings into an untidy kitchen, through a middle room and into the front one. A glance around indicated it was the largest room in the house. It appeared smallest though, because a double bed stood in one corner and a convertible leather davenport in the other. A dresser, several chairs, and an old upright piano crowded the remaining space. The bird dog had shed hair over everything, including the beds. Sunlight slanted through a fly-specked window, revealing a faded pattern on the threadbare carpet.

Mrs. Smith plumped down her bulk on the davenport, the springs creaking and pinging as though in protest, and heaved an expansive sigh. Carrie primly sat in a straight-backed chair because it looked cleaner than the others.

So this would be her home for the next seven months! She felt her heart sinking into her polished, button shoes. How could she ever put up with the filth? But she was broke, and beggars couldn't be choosers, although it did seem a hard fate to have her boarding place settled without consulting her. She was still too inexperienced in the ways of the world to assert herself.

Sadie,* as Mrs. Smith insisted on being called — a habit of the country, Carrie had observed, as everyone from youngsters to grandparents called one another by given names or nicknames — proved to be an Irish woman from Kentucky who had been favored with a fair education. While they rested in the dingy front room, she told Carrie that she had adopted three orphan children. Their Swedish mother had died giving birth to her fourteenth child. Two of the children were Minnie and Maria. The third, four-year-old Earl, a pale, sickly child suffering from rickets, lay asleep on the bed.

"At suppertime," Carrie said, "I met Denny, Sadie's husband. Like her father, Denny was a small, dried-up sort of man only younger. I thought him the homeliest person I had ever seen. His nose had been frozen one winter, leaving a knob of bone which gave him a monkey-like appearance.

"When bedtime came, I began speculating about sleeping arrangements for four adults and three children in two rooms.

---

* *True name forgotten.*

Chapter 4 — Trials and Tribulations of a Country Schoolma'am

" 'I'm rather tired,' I hinted to Sadie and got up from the kitchen table where the four of us had been playing cards, 'so if you'll tell where my bed is —.' "

"Time we was all turnin' in," Sadie agreed, and heaved herself out of the chair. "C'mon and I'll show ye."

While they were passing through the middle room, Sadie motioned with the lamp toward the bed and explained, "Pa and Denny bed down there." The bird dog was already curled up on a rag rug.

In the front room Carrie noticed the three children fast asleep on the davenport, which had been opened into a bed.

After she placed the lamp on the piano top, Sadie gestured toward the iron double bed. "That's where me an' you'll hit the hay."

"Unbelieving for a moment, I stared at her in horror, wondering what space would be left after Sadie's three-hundred pounds had been disposed of." Carrie laughed at the memory.

Misinterpreting the look, Sadie said tartly, "Well, this ain't no city hotel. What'd you expect — a pink boodwar?"

Blushing, Carrie hastily assured her everything would be all right. She understood that country people had to make the best of things, because she was one of them herself.

No sooner had Sadie turned in than she began to snore loudly in varying keys and pitches. Carrie clung precariously to the bed's edge, thinking she'd sooner have a buzz-saw for a sleeping mate. If Sadie would let some of this nocturnal noise escape through open windows it would be a bit of comfort. But her principles didn't approve the admission of night air. Carrie set her mind to scheming a way out of the dilemma, and desperately decided Sadie must be waked up long enough for her to get to sleep. She stuck her feet outside the covers until they grew icy cold, then put them against Sadie. Abruptly, the snoring ended in a startled snort. Carrie prayed she would quickly drop off now in the blessed silence.

On the opening day of school, a crisp, bright blue October morning, Old Man Petrie told Carrie he'd take her over in style.

After breakfast he hitched the skinny team to the buckboard and Carrie, Petrie, and the two girls rattled northwest over the prairie for two miles to the third homesteader's shack, a two-story, unpainted house falling into ruins. Bare of shrubbery or trees, its uncurtained windows stared vacantly upon the ripe grass. Some distance behind the house Carrie saw a pump and water trough near a ramshackle barn. They drove into the fenced yard and Petrie pulled up the horses.

"This here's it," he said. "Arneberg's place. His four boys'll be your scholars. Good luck to ye."

He turned the team about and started home as Carrie, followed by Minnie and Maria, walked up to the porchless, sagging front door. She was glad Sis wasn't here to ridicule "Carrie's school," or Bill to see her sickhearted disillusion.

If only she could flop down in the dried grass and have a good cry, she imagined she'd feel better. But the little girls, trustfully tagging her, would think her silly and unworthy of their respect. The worst must be faced. She had never yet laid down and quit. If these poor little young 'uns could take it, she certainly could.

Taking a deep breath and squaring her shoulders, Carrie forced open the door and stepped into a large, bare room, furnished with a few battered, knife-carved desks and an old table that served as the teacher's desk. Glancing about, she could discover no books, no blackboard, no paper or supplies of any kind, nor any cupboard where supplies could be stored. At her left was a doorway opening into the kitchen. Waves of heated air came from the fire in the wood-burning stove and faintly lingering, greasy odors of food from breakfast. Carrie heard sounds of scuffling and boys' voices in the attic. Such abject poverty she had never seen. A tremor of nausea went through her. Then a conjecture became suddenly a conviction. She turned to Minnie, who stood in the open doorway.

"Oh, your mother was Mrs. Arneberg, and this is where she — " Carrie caught herself in time. Arneberg's wife was the Swedish woman who had died in her fourteenth childbirth, she recalled. Perhaps she had passed away in this very room.

Chapter 4 — Trials and Tribulations of a Country Schoolma'am

"Tex" Stalling's 12-horse freight outfit, the "Jerk-line 12 on the old North Montana freight road along Sunday Creek to and from the small settlements not served by the railroad was hauled by such outfits as this in the early 1900s. This one had an 85-mile haul and made one round trip each week in good weather." (Courtesy, Coffrin's Old West Gallery, Miles City, from L. A. Huffman photo.)

"Yes'm, Ma used ter live here, but she died," Minnie explained with childish candor.

"Oh." Disconcerted, Carrie quickly changed the subject, asking where were the schoolbooks and the blackboard?

"They ain't none."

"There *aren't any*," Carrie corrected.

Minnie looked up at teacher with a guileless stare. "Yes'm, but there ain't."

To hide her smile, Carrie tapped her teeth with her thumbnail and turned her head. So much had to be done, she hardly knew where to begin. Dust and shavings littered the floor, and the desks were all askew. Little Maria was trying out each desk to find one to fit her first grade size.

As Carrie laid her notebooks, pencils, lunch box, and her own favorite reader on the table, she told Minnie to call the boys down. They could help clean up the room.

Minnie skipped across to the stairway and shouted up, "C'mon down, kids! Teacher's here!"

Heavy shoes noisily clumped down the wooden stairs and two tow-headed boys in overalls burst into the schoolroom. They stopped at sight of Carrie and critically sized her up.

"Gee, she's pretty!" the smaller boy whispered to his brother, eyeing the teacher's black hair and red dotted swiss dress.

"Good morning, boys," she greeted them, a blush spreading over her face. She decided to ignore the compliment and asked their names.

"I'm Tuffy," the older one, sturdy and good-looking, replied.

"I'm Oscar." He was paler and smaller than his brother.

"Tuffy?" Carrie raised her heavy eyebrows.

"Yeah," Oscar supplied, "his name's Robert, but we call 'im Tuffy 'cause he's allus shootin' off guns in the yard."

"Aw, shut up!" Tuffy commanded.

Carrie stared at Tuffy in what she hoped was her most severe schoolteacherish manner. "There'll be no shooting of guns in the schoolyard while I'm teacher here, young man." Relaxing then, she inquired conversationally, "How old are you, Robert?"

Oscar giggled at the queer sound of his brother's proper name, and the girls joined in. Tuffy scowled.*

"I'm twelve an' Oscar's 'leven."

"What were you making all that noise upstairs about?"

"Aw," Oscar spoke up, "Carl told us to make the beds. He's boss."

"Where is he and your other brother?"

"Him an' Eric's down to the barn. Tendin' stock."

"Go call them, Oscar. They'll have to help clean up the schoolroom." As Oscar ran out, slamming the door, Carrie turned to Tuffy. "Robert, you get a broom, a mop, some hot water, and soap. Minnie and Maria, you girls find old rags for dustcloths."

While the children obediently went about their tasks, Carrie heard the front door close softly and turned from her desk to see a neatly dressed little girl with pigtails braided around her head standing quietly inside.

"My goodness, another pupil! And what's your name?"

The newcomer informed the teacher that she was Norma Dixon, seven years old and in the second grade.

Carrie offered Norma a rag, saying she could help dust.

By noon, under the supervision of the serious-minded, 15-year-old Carl, aided by his 13½-year-old brother Eric, the room was scrubbed and arranged to Carrie's satisfaction.

"I decided to spend the afternoon teaching the children by talking and reading to them. Indeed, this routine was followed until supplies were forthcoming from the school board in Miles City. Later, a schoolhouse was built at the 12-Mile Bridge Road and was the center of social life for the area. Elections, dances,

---

* One old-timer recalled that Ray Lowe, a rancher friend of the Nichols family, "informally adopted one of the Arneberg boys and he was called Tuffy Lowe. I think he served in the Marines during World War I. In these later years Tuffy lived at Coarse Gold, California, south of Fresno. His health was very bad" (Walter E. Mann, Letter to author, November 14, 1981).

and basket socials were all held there" (*Fanning the Embers*, p. 364).

After getting better acquainted with her pupils, Carrie found the Arneberg youngsters without exception smart and eager to learn, although Sadie always referred to their father as a good-for-nothing so-and-so. After his wife's death, she told Carrie, he had gone to Miles to work and left his four oldest sons to shift for themselves, while he proceeded to drink up his wages. For weeks at a time the boys went without nourishing food or fuel in the dead of winter. Occasionally, his conscience pricked him and he would haul out a wagon load of groceries, only to disappear for another indefinite period.

Were it not for the generosity of neighboring homesteaders who willingly chipped in to donate food, clothing, and wood, the young Arnebergs couldn't have kept body and soul together. As it was, their fuel was always short, and many a day that winter Carrie had to teach school without a fire. The thermometer hovered around zero or dropped below. "Whoever believed that pioneering days were over by 1912 and 1913, I frequently told myself, should have visited my school for a few weeks."

That first day she dismissed classes early. While waiting for Old Man Petrie to come with the buckboard, she watched the boys play one-o'-cat ball. When he failed to appear in an hour and it was getting on toward suppertime, Carrie called Minnie and Maria and began tramping the two miles to the Smith homestead. She enjoyed the walk in the mellow, late afternoon sun, but was afraid six-year-old Maria might become fatigued. The sisters skipped about her, talking at random and picking late blooming flowers by the dusty roadside, which they held up in grimy little fists for her inspection and admiration.

When she reached the kitchen door, Carrie seemed more tired than the girls. Before she could open the screen, Sadie pushed it violently outward and stood in the doorway, hands on hips. She had a pugnacious glitter in her eyes and reminded Carrie of a bellicose hen with ruffled feathers.

Carrie stepped back in blank surprise.

"I might's well tell ya," Sadie informed her in truculent tones, " 'cause ye'll find it out anyhow. I jist beat up Denny an' knocked two of his teeth out, an' I give Pa a good larrupin', too."

Oh!" Carrie gasped. "What — what — was the trouble?"

"Denny, the god damn bastard, was drinkin' with a freight outfit all afternoon, an' meself countin' pennies and slavin' day in an' day out to raise another drunkard's brats. Them low, no 'count teamsters!" she spat into the dust at Carrie's feet. "He come home reelin' an' whinin' an' callin' me Babe this an' Babe that. Well, ain't nobody 'lowed to call me that, 'cept Pa, so I waded into 'im. Then Pa got smart an' stuck his nose in, too, so I lets 'im have it. . . . Men!" she scoffed, and waddled back into the kitchen.

"Next time he goes on a spree, I'll car-r-ve his damn heart out," she growled menacingly from within.

She would try to do it, too, Carrie learned. On other occasions when Denny came home intoxicated, Sadie chased him around the table with a carving knife, threatening to "cut his damn guts out." Denny, dodging the wildly brandished weapon, pleaded with her to be reasonable, but only when she was out of breath did she give up the chase. Then she had to "set a spell" and wheeze.

Carrie shivered, wondering whether the woman might be mentally unstable. It was always well to humor her during these outbursts of rage, although they seemed to pass as suddenly as they came. Carrie kept constantly on guard, though, to avoid raising Sadie's ire.

After supper, eaten in a grimly silent atmosphere, Carrie felt so lonely and discouraged that if she could have found any privacy she would have relieved her nervous tension from the day's trials in a fit of weeping. Instead, she wrote a letter to the school board, reporting on conditions, and then expressed heartfelt misery in a long letter to Bill, telling him not to say anything to Sis. Tears splashed onto the paper, blurring the ink. Too weary and forlorn to recopy it, she placed the stained letter in the mailbox the next morning.

"As I trudged off to school, Minnie and Maria playing games 'round me, I seriously considered resigning my job. But where could I go? Back to Sis' place? Or worse still, back to my father's house in Wisconsin? I gritted my teeth and tightly shut my eyes to hold back the tears. Somehow I must find strength and courage to see it through. And I needed the money to pay back what I had borrowed from High-Pockets for the trip to Miles. After that debt was paid, I'd start saving for the little sod shanty in the West that Bill and I had planned.

"Well, today was another day, I told myself, and after all, I *had* lived through the ordeal of yesterday. If only Sadie wouldn't throw another angry tantrum!"

Chapter 5

A Dashing Lochinvar and Showdown with Sadie 1912-1913

A few days after school opened, Carrie returned home to find Sadie preparing supper and talking to what seemed to her a middleaged man with a dark complexion, black hair, gray eyes, and a black mustache. As Carrie entered the kitchen, he jumped to his feet and gave her a slight bow. How chivalrous of him, she thought, noting his slim, wiry body, gracefully proportioned to his medium height. Although he wore the usual stockman's working clothes — unbuttoned vest, woolen pants, and black riding boots — Carrie suspected him of being vain. A colorful horsehair hatband decorated the black hat held in his hand.

"Here's the new schoolma'am," Sadie introduced her. "Carrie, meet Smokey Nichols. He rode by to look you over."

Carrie felt the blood rush to her face at Sadie's blunt statement, but she managed to murmur the social amenities. He smiled disarmingly and she caught the gleam of white teeth.

Quickly, she marshaled the gossip that Sadie had already told her about this rancher of wild reputation. Owner of the UY Ranch, mostly a horse outfit, he was divorced and had two sons. He was also reputed to be quick-tempered and handy with a sixgun, like most men who had grown up on the frontier. Of presumed Spanish descent, he was considered quite a lady's man because of his charming Hispanic manners. But to her nineteen years his forty-four appeared rather venerable.

She laid her books on the faded oil tablecloth and sat in the chair he pulled up for her

After an exchange of pleasantries he asked in a soft Texas drawl, "how y'all get back and forth to school? Shank's mare?"

Sometimes Mr. Petrie drove them, she explained, and sometimes they rode the team. Mostly they walked.

"Pa ain't got time to gallivant to school ev'ry day," Sadie interjected from the stove where she was stirring some concoction which, strangely enough, had an appetizing odor.

Smokey kept his eyes on the teacher, ignoring Sadie's interruption, as he asked if she would like a saddle horse of her own.

"It would be nice."

He had a "bunch of broom-tail cayuses eatin' their heads off," and he'd be glad to loan her one. There was a little bay, name of Brownie, "well broke" and gentle enough for a lady to handle. He "reckoned" he could rustle up a saddle, too.

Carrie thanked him, although his offer troubled her.

"That's very nice of you, but I'm afraid the folks here don't have any extra hay." She had noticed Sadie stiffen and half turn toward her.

Smokey brushed aside that objection, saying he'd have one of the boys haul over a wagon load. . . . "By the way, what size boot do y'all take?" He stared down appraisingly at her black button shoes, now grayish from the roadside dust.

Carrie laughed to hide her embarrassment. But she held up five fingers. Smokey nodded. Later, he told her he had bet a gallon of whiskey with one of his cowboys that the new teacher would not wear over a number three shoe.

Suddenly remembering the gossip Sadie had told her, Carrie asked Smokey why his sons were not coming to school.

Smokey gave her a sidelong glance and said off-handedly that Bub, his oldest boy, finished school; he was going on 17. Dutch was younger and "livin' with his ma in Milestown."

Chapter 5 — A Dashing Lochinvar and Showdown with Sadie

Before he left Smokey promised to have one of the boys round up Brownie and turn him into the pasture, so she'd have him to ride in a day or so.

A saddle horse for her own use meant recreation and new independence for Carrie. On Saturday afternoons and Sundays she began to take long rides over the prairie and investigate the old abandoned Indian camps along the creeks, where the children told her they had found stone knives and arrowheads. This whole region, she had learned, was once a Sioux and Cheyenne hunting ground. Some distance up North Sunday Creek, beyond the UY Ranch, was the old "Dry House" where hide hunters once cured buffalo meat.

Brownie proved to be all that his owner had claimed, and she quickly grew fond of the steady-going little bay. Furthermore, he had no objections to bearing an extra burden, so Minnie and Maria were able to ride double behind the saddle.

After the generous loan of the pony, Smokey made a point of riding by on crisp, autumn mornings and accompanying Carrie to school. She encouraged him to talk about himself and his ranch, for he had a romantic background. Bit by bit she pieced it all together. His grandfather, at age three, had been rescued from a wrecked Spanish vessel found somewhere in the Atlantic Ocean. All the child could say was, "big guns shoot." The mystery of that ill-fated ship was never solved. A family in South Carolina took the baby and reared him to manhood. His son, William Henry Nichols, born August 26, 1840, in Dry Ridge, Grant County, Kentucky, located on a farm in Illinois and married Martha Shoots, a native of that state. There Smokey was born.* As a rebellious boy of 13 who didn't want to go to school, he ran away from home and "beat his way" to Texas.

The free, roving life of the cowboy attracted him, and soon he

---

* *Smokey's birth place was also given as Ohio in the 1900 U. S. Census, and as Kansas in Saul F. "Dutch" Nichols' death certificate. Some relatives doubt Smokey's "grandfather" story.*

was following the "Long Drive," once called the Texas or Northern Trail of longhorns. The first Montana horses he saw looked like elephants, he said, because they were so much bigger than the small mustangs of the Southwest plains. He soon decided to settle down in the north. In time he acquired the UY horse ranch and some cattle. He was now doing a profitable business selling remounts to the cavalry stationed at Fort Keogh and to farmers, he assured Carrie.

"Like to dance?" he asked one morning as they rode along the fenced track on the way to school. Frost still whitened the ripe blades of prairie grass, though the sun was high.

"I'd love to — only my father never permitted me to learn how." It embarrassed her to admit it. But if she pretended otherwise she would lose his respect when he found out, and she wanted to stand high in his esteem.

Smokey looked curiously at her, and said her education had to be improved "pronto." He'd teach her at the "shindig next Sat'day over on South Sunday Crick."

The invitation thrilled Carrie. She would write Bill explaining matters, and he would understand. If she said nothing and he learned about it from others, he would naturally think she was two-timing on him.

"From then on," Carrie related, "I went to all the dances with Smokey because I wanted to forget the dirt at the Smith homestead. And he was my one social contact. Of course, I had an occasional dinner and spent the night at the Dixon home. Always, I was loath to leave their tidy house. Each time I did accept an invitation, though, Sadie apparently resented it and made nasty digs like, 'was common folks not good 'nough for me?'

"Things generally started going from bad to worse at my boarding place. Every letter I received from home or from Sis was crumpled and the flap scarcely sealed. When a long letter from Sis had one of the pages folded in new creases, I suspected Sadie was opening and reading my mail while while I was away at school."

Chapter 5 — A Dashing Lochinvar and Showdown with Sadie

Such effrontery emboldened Carrie to intimate on that occasion that it was mighty funny that every letter she got was all mussed up. She stared pointedly at Sadie, whose fat face reddened.

She tossed the strands of hair out of her eyes and retorted, "Well, d'ye think the mailman's got time to read all the letters on the way up from Miles? Or maybe ye think I got nothin' to do but pry into your affairs? Is that it, my purty miss? 'Pears to me you're gittin' mighty highhanded of late, always chasin' 'round with that old duck Smokey." She gave the dough she was kneading a spiteful punch. "He's nothin' but a lady-killer, even it he does own a horse ranch. Mind my words, for I'm a-warnin' ye."

Only distaste for quarreling kept sharp words from leaving Carrie's mouth. Instead she said with prim dignity that in her company Smokey was always a gentleman, and buried her face in Sis' letter again. The baby had come, an eight-and-a-half pound boy. "George is so crazy about him he is already planning to buy him a pair of chaps and a pinto pony," the letter ran. They only reference to Bill was in a postscript: "Billy is away on the beef roundup, so he has not yet seen his new nephew. Wonder how he will like being 'Uncle Billy' as we have been calling him?"

That was why she hadn't heard from him, Carrie consoled herself. Ranch work had kept him too busy to write. Men were so careless about such things. When the first week passed and no letter came, she had felt neglected, but when three weeks went by without even a postcard, she grew depressed and all the more willing to encourage Smokey's attentions. How foolish she had been to take it so hard. Surely she would hear by Christmas after roundup time.

As weeks rolled by and the brown prairie became whitened by winter snows, Carrie had to force herself into the Christmas spirit for the sake of Sadie's adopted children. A leaden weight seemed to hang in her breast. The spring had gone out of her ankles and even teaching, which she enjoyed, became a dull and routine task. Her lively curiosity regarding the novel life about her dimmed, and then faded into indifference. Love's inspiration no longer burned brightly, for not a single letter had arrived from Bill, although she recalled, "I heard about him indirectly now and then from ranchers who occasionally dropped in to the Smiths. Sis' last letter had described what good times he was having, and how popular he was at dances with his 'nice singing voice.'

"The news drove me to the bitter conclusion that he had found another girl. Perhaps he was mad at me for going to dances with Smokey. But if he intended to jilt me, why didn't he do the decent thing — write and properly break our engagement? Or return my letters? Pride kept me from sending word by stockmen back to him, or from going over at Christmas to find out what had happened, so I endured my heartbreak in martyred silence. I had finally given up writing to him. But I still had Smokey. He had taken no other girl to a dance since we started going together. Didn't that prove his devoted interest?"

At the holiday season Carrie made a painful decision. She would put faithless Bill out of mind, forget her own troubles, and try to bring a little cheer into the lives of others. She took part of last month's salary and bought warm clothing for the seven young Arnebergs. Together she and the Smiths planned a celebration, but then Denny went to town on Christmas Eve for a celebration of his own, and Sadie determined to follow him.

"And I'll car-r-ve him in two if I git hold of him," she snarled.

"You probably couldn't find him if you did go to Miles," Carrie objected, "and anyway you promised the kids a Christmas. I need your help to candy apples and string popcorn balls. And no one can roast a goose quite as nicely as you did on Thanksgiving. Wait till after the holidays," she went on, watching Sadie beam with pleasure over the compliment. "Think how disappointed the four Arneberg boys will be, if you go."

Sadie relented but promised to give Denny a double beating when he got back.

Christmas Day passed pleasantly enough for Carrie because her pupils enjoyed their dinner and presents so, but the dirt and obscene language at the Smith homestead frayed her nerves during the vacation. She had planned to spend the holidays with Bill at Sis' place. Instead she was eating her heart out for a man who never gave her a thought.

Then came the invitation to the New Year's dance at the Campbells'.* That meant a few hours' release from her purgatory. During New Year's eve afternoon, she went happily about the shack making preparations while Sadie watched her in glum disapproval.

When Smokey called to take her to the dance, she eagerly buttoned a mackinaw over her riding skirt and stuffed a woolen dress into the saddlebags. As they left the house, Sadie was silent.

Smokey rode beside Carrie on his favorite horse, a chunky brown named Music. Although the snow was not deep, the sharpening cold in the air and a sullen gray sky hinted at a storm. A rising north wind struck in icy puffs, nipping their faces, fingers, and toes. The horses' breath immediately froze, frosting muzzles and shoulders. The snow gave off a dry, creaking sound at each hoofstep.

Smokey remarked, squinting at the sky, it wouldn't surprise him if a blizzard was making up. Small icicles had formed on his mustache.

Carrie shivered as cold air penetrated her clothing. She wouldn't care if she never got back, she complained.

Smokey asked if Sadie had been "on the prod again?"

"Not more than usual, but she keeps that house so filthy dirty the pigs would spurn it. Do you know she hasn't even taken a bath since the warm weather in October. And you'd think I was committing a crime when I insisted on having mine. To cap the climax, the other day I finally caught her steaming open one of my letters. It's not the first time she's done that. . . . I'm sorry, I

---

* *True name forgotten.*

didn't mean to weep on your shoulder with my troubles," she apologized. "But everything there has been getting on my nerves so, I can't bear the thought of going back."

"Shore," Smokey sympathized. "Why don't yuh move out on her?"

"She'd throw fifty-seven varieties of fits. That's the trouble. She thinks she owns me body and soul and has a right to pry into my business. Her latest has been trying to match me with that shiftless brother of hers, who's always chewing tobacco."

Smokey wiped icicles off his mustache on back of his gauntlet and prophesied, one of these days she'd have a showdown with Sadie, and the sooner the better. "Don't let her spook yuh, little girl." He gave her a warm, encouraging grin.

Early dusk was falling as they rode up the lane to the neat Campbell homestead. The cheery glow of lamplight shone through the windows, and the sound of boisterous talk and laughter floated outdoors. A few flakes of snow began to drift lazily down from lowering clouds while they rode on to the stable. Carrie noticed an assortment of spring wagons and buckboards near the barn and a number of saddle horses munching hay in the corral. Evidently homesteaders, ranchers and their wives had already braved the threat of a coming storm to enjoy the square dances and two-steps. Smokey unsaddled the horses and found a vacant tie-stall in the barn for them.

When they entered the living room, the floor was already filled with dancers capering to the offkey tune of "The Gal with the Balmoral," played by an "orchestra" of fiddles and a squeaky accordion. The women wore their best woolen dresses, the long skirts sweeping the floor; the men had put on polished black boots and clean shirts, sleeked their hair back and shaved their faces. One husky farmer espied Carrie, still in her riding skirt, grabbed her and whirled her off with a grin. Smokey stood by smiling, saddlebags tucked under one arm, and hands clapping in time to the music.

When refreshment time arrived, Carrie sat between Smokey and her hostess near the cast-iron heating stove. Shorty, an uninvited guest, came striding in, his manner purposeful. Abruptly all chatting ceased. Snowflakes powdered his sourdough (sheepskin) coat and an aura of cold air surrounded him. His eyes glittered with excitement, Carrie noticed on looking up from the plate in her lap. She recognized him as a cowboy from a ranch near Smokey's range.

Shorty greeted the merrymakers, then said to Carrie in a low voice, "Kin I talk to yuh a minit — alone?"

"Why, certainly." Surprised, she excused herself, and led him into the kitchen. She had changed into a dark plaid dress with a high neck, long sleeves and flaring skirt. Her hair had been piled on top of her head, giving a pompadour effect and making her look older, the impression desired because of sensitivity over the disparity between Smokey's age and hers.

"I jist heerd somethin' I think yuh oughta know about," Shorty began in a confidential tone.

"What in the world!"

Shorty said he had dropped in to see Old Man Petrie and had asked Sadie about the teacher. And did Carrie know what Sadie had the "gol-darn nerve to insin-u-ate?" He paused doubtless relishing the dramatic effect of his words on Carrie's perplexed countenance. "Sadie said the teacher rode off with Smokey some while ago." He continued, " 'They *said* they was goin' to Campbell's dance,' she said. Them's her eggsact words. So I come here like a devil was tailin' me, jist so's I could prove you *was* here. An' if she starts any scandal 'bout yuh, you bein' teacher an' all, I'll stick up for yuh."

Carrie exploded in indignation. Then, controlling her righteous anger, she told Shorty to come tell Mrs. Campbell and Smokey what he'd just told her, in case the tale got back to the school board. He licked his lips, no doubt pleased over being the center of attention.

When Shorty had repeated the gossip, Smokey muttered profanely under his breath, and Mrs. Campbell, a neat, darkhaired woman with a pink and white complexion, sputtered indignantly.

"I think that's terrible," Carrie fumed, her cheeks flaming. "Imagine her nerve saying such things about me behind my back."

"Never mind, lassie," the hostess comforted her, pointing out she had plenty of witnesses to alibi for her and adding that the fiddlers were tuning up for a waltz. "You and Smokey enjoy yourselves now. . . . Shorty, help yourself to some grub."

In a few minutes the orchestra was blaring again, but the sudden roar of the wind, howling round the house, muffled the sound of music. Carrie took a wicked delight in the blizzard because she would have to stay until dawn. That would really give Sadie something to rave about!

Next day, though, the wind continued to blow full-blast over the prairie and most guests were obliged to spend another night. The men rolled up in blankets on the floor of one room, the women in another. But the people made a joke of their imprisonment, and nothing could shake their good nature and holiday mood. They laughed, played cards, danced, drank hot toddies, and told stories, only stopping while the men tied ropes around each other and fought their way out to the barn through the storm's blinding, white fury to tend the stock.

In the morning the silence was like a void, so great was the contrast to the world-filling noise of the last 36 hours. Carrie and Smokey left right after breakfast so that she could be on time to open the school. But snow had drifted so deeply in places they were already an hour late when they reached the Smith house. The buildings' chinks, cracks, and window ledges were plastered with snow. their unpainted boards were a drab sight in the blank white waste surrounding them. A thin plume of smoke rose from the chimney. The pair reined in the horses at the open wire gate.

Carrie told Smokey she'd better go in and find out if Sadie had already sent the girls to school. If they hadn't left yet, she wouldn't hold classes today.

"There's a little matter to be settled between her and me." A reluctant, sinking feeling came over Carrie.

Chapter 5 — A Dashing Lochinvar and Showdown with Sadie

Smokey grinned in appreciation, "Need any help?"

"No, thanks, I can handle this alone." Carrie waved to him and trotted the bay pony up to the kitchen door. Intent on the matter confronting her, she was unaware that Smokey was riding only very slowly along the road. She dropped the reins in the snow and stamped inside.

Minnie was at the table cutting paper dolls from a mailorder catalogue, and Maria, humming to herself, was sorting them out. Four-year-old Earl was beating a Christmas-present drum.

"Where's Sadie?"

Minnie tossed her head. "Ma's over at Dixons," she answered in an insolent tone, "and she said I didn't hafta go t'school to no teacher what stays away all night with Smokey."

The child's taunt fired anew Carrie's indignation. This time Sadie had "plumb overstepped her reach," in the cowboy vernacular.

Carrie said grimly she'd see about that, and going out slammed the kitchen door. Swinging into the saddle, she dug heels into Brownie's ribs. Surprised, the pony leaped into a gallop and only stopped when Carrie jerked him back on his haunches at the Dixon homestead, south of the UY at what was called the 12-Mile Bridge Road Ranch.

The Dixons were plain, wholesome people from the Midwest, and their orderly place had always seemed a paradise to Carrie. She had a fleeting impression of leafless cottonwood trees around the house, and of the well-kept yard. But she was too perturbed to be more than vaguely conscious of details, or to notice a rider coming southward. Leaping from the saddle, she paused long enough to knock on the kitchen door, then entered.

Sadie, sitting by the table, a shapeless heap, had a smug expression on her fat face. Evaline Dixon, washing the breakfast dishes which Norma was drying, appeared distressed and flustered upon recognizing Carrie. Norma stared open-mouthed at teacher's snapping eyes, and held plate and tea cloth suspended in midair.

Without a word of greeting Carrie strode up to Sadie, whose

eyes flew open and jaw hung slack. Hands on hips, she began speaking in a low, tense voice, "I defy you to prove the nasty scandal you started about me! Ask the Campbells if it's true. Ask the people who were with me during the blizzard. Ask Shorty."

She threatened to have Sadie arrested for defaming her character and told Sadie she was fed up with her dirty house and filthy mouth. Her voice rose in pitch as all the bitterness, wretchedness, heartbreak, and loneliness of the past months found acid-edged expression and literally struck Sadie dumb. Carrie later told Smokey that Sadie was probably more astounded at a slim, young girl tongue-lashing her, than at the things she said.

To cap it all, Carrie concluded, rather breathlessly, Sadie was guilty of opening her private mail. She had caught her steaming the last letter over the teakettle — the one Sadie *said* got wet in the mailbox. Then her voice broke, and through angry tears she cried, half-hysterically, "I'm moving out — you hear? I don't know where I'll go, but I won't spend another night in your pigpen!"

Evaline Dixon, a cheerful woman in a starched apron, put her arms around the sobbing, trembling teacher. "There, there, dearie, never mind. You can stay with us." She'd send Walt over to fetch Carrie's things, and told Norma to run down to the barn and tell her father to hitch the sleigh.

As Norma slipped into her coat and ran out, Sadie got ponderously to her feet, her eyes narrowing.

She jeered at "the chit" calling her a criminal and threatened to make Carrie "eat your words, my purty miss, ye little God —."

"Sadie!" Evaline Dixon sharply exclaimed. "You'd better leave before you stick your foot in any further. Can't you see the girl's all upset?"

Sadie gave her a chilling stare. "I kin see I'm not wanted here any more." Savagely she pulled on her coat, and whirled toward Carrie. "Tis a horsewhippin' I'll be a givin' ye —." She broke off as Smokey and Walter Dixon walked through the doorway.

In his drawl Smokey asked her who was going to horsewhip who? Suddenly, his voice snapped words at her like the crack of a bullwhip, "Sadie, I and Walt jist heard yo' threat. If yuh harm a single hair of Carrie's haid, we'll see y'all put behind bars. Don't forget." But Sadie had gone out, muttering to herself and slamming the door.

Again in a mild drawl he spoke to Carrie, "She's put the Injun sign on yuh for fair. I'll feel a heap safer for yuh from now on, if I or one of the boys sees y'all to and from school. Some one of my boys goin' to become yo' star pupil till the term ends — jist in case that jughead tries to tie into yuh durin' school hours."

Carrie gave Smokey a tear-bright but warm smile, expressing heartfelt gratitude for his kindness and protection. How absurd of Sadie to warn her against him!

* * *

Bruce Mott, a retired cattle and horse rancher from west of Miles City on Moon Creek, wrote the author on Oct. 20, 1981: "Evaline Dixon was related to my grandmother Elizabeth Huff Mott on my father's side of the family. My grandmother died here in Miles City in 1918.

"Walter Dixon and his wife Evaline filed on a homestead on North Sunday Creek around 1908 or 1909. Their place was located at the 12 mile crossing on the old stage road. They obtained some income from running a road house. I don't believe they engaged in farming or the stock business to any great extent." In a telephone interview (October 4, 1981), Mr. Mott was unable to recall the Dixons' daughter's name.

Mr. Mott was born in Miles City, April 3, 1901. His parents, C. H. (Larry) and Helen J. Henry Mott "had a modest ranching enterprise on the Yellowstone at the mouth of Moon Creek" (*Fanning the Embers*, p. 300), where his father kept a small herd of buffalo. Between 1912 and 1920, C. H. Mott served as mayor of Miles City in addition to other civic offices. His son Bruce took a year out from capturing escaped buffalo to act as secretary-treasurer of Range Riders, Inc.

Chapter 6

The UY's Colorful Boss

Earl W. "Smokey" Nichols was a well-known horse rancher on Miles City's "north side," as the area north of the Yellowstone River was called. Indeed, Carrie recalled: "Everyone knew Smokey Nichols, from Teddy Roosevelt to the itinerant puncher."

Like the gaps in Carrie's reminiscences for the remainder of the school year, there are likewise many gaps in Smokey's history before he met the "new schoolma'am." Background material from public documents includes some puzzling discrepancies. For instance, his death certificate, filed in the Bureau of Vital Statistics, Helena, Montana, states: "Full name: Earl Wilbur Nichols; male, white, married; birthdate: March 19, 1878; age 53 years, one month, 22 days; deceased's occupation: Rancher; birthplace: Ill." (Information furnished by Bud [sic] Nichols).

However, two errors herein became obvious when checked with other data. "Bud" was Bub, Smokey's oldest son, christened Earl William Nichols, according to Bub's wife, Mrs. Margaret Mann Nichols. In Smokey's last will, written May 10, 1921, the day before he died, Smokey gave his age as 53. If 1878 was his correct birth date, he would have been 43 at his death. In a long distance telephone interview, Tom Colleran, secretary of

Earl Willard "Smokey" Nichols, the handsome UY-Rafter T horse rancher on Miles City's "north side." Taken 1913 in Miles City by Albert Schlichtins (who became Carrie's third husband.) (Courtesy, his granddaughter, Betty Grayce Nichols Kalfell.)

the Range Riders Museum in Miles City, told the writer in April 1980 that he knew Smokey and grew up with his sons. He believed the UY boss was several years older than 43 in 1921. Thus, 1868 should be Smokey's correct date of birth for age 53 at death. Smokey's "correct name was Earl *Willard* Nichols," Bub's widow informed the writer in a letter, August 24, 1980. His mother was an admirer of Frances Willard, a 19th century American philanthropist and temperance advocate. Smokey's granddaughter, Nora Nichols (Mrs. Hugh Randolph), wrote on August 7, 1980, that her grandfather had seven brothers and sisters, all of whom have died.

An inexplicable variation in Smokey's presumed vital statistics was discovered in the 1900 Federal Census for Montana in which the birthdate of an "Earl Nichols" was listed as April 1865; his age 35; his marital status single; his birthplace Ohio; and his occupation farm laborer. Possibly, were there two Earl Nichols residing in Montana in 1900?

It would seem so, because the Miles City *Star* (January 4, 1917) noted in a local news column: "Earl Nichols is in the city from Fallon." Below this item was: "Smoky [sic] Nichols, who is in from his ranch on the north side, says that stock looks good and that there has been very little feeding done yet by anyone."*

Another oddity appeared in *The Montana Stock Grower's Directory, Marks and Brands*, 1888-1900, which recorded the UY brand to Mrs. E. W. Nichols, Fallon, Montana, with both cattle and horse brands on left shoulder. Smokey's marriage was confirmed in a Complaint issued by the district Court of the Seventh Judicial District of the State of Montana, in and for the County of Custer, for Earl W. Nichols, Plaintiff, vs. Anna Nichols, Defendant, which stated: "That the plaintiff and the defendant were married on the 20th day of December, 1894, at Glendive, in the County of Dawson, State of Montana, and ever since then have been, and now are, husband and wife." This document was "Subscribed and sworn to before me this 15th day of October, A. D. 1907," George W. Farr, Notary Public in and for Custer County, Montana. Mr. Farr became Smokey's attorney.

Another unexplained recording in the *Annual Reports* of the Board of Stock Commissioners, the state Veterinarian, and the Recorder of Mark [sic] and Brands, of the State of Montana, for the year 1904 listed the UY brand in "Mrs. Anna Nichols" name, in Miles City, Custer County, with "Brand for cattle on left shoulder. . . . Transferred from E. W. Nichols." The reason for the transfer has not been learned by the writer. However, the *Brand Book* of the Montana Stock Growers' Association for

---

* *Bub's widow states that there "were not two Earl Nichols," excluding, of course, her husband (Earl W. Nichols), and she did not identify the Earl Nichols from Fallon as her bridegroom of six months.*

Anna Egan Nichols, Smokey's first wife, on left, with her elder daughter, Nora, taken in a Texas oil field after Nora's high school graduation in Miles City. Smokey financed the trip as a gift for Nora to visit her mother. (Courtesy, Mrs. Margaret Mann Nichols.)

1910 recorded the UY brand for horses on "left shoulder" and four other brands for cattle in E. W. Nichols name, "P.O. address, Miles City, Montana."*

In *Fanning the Embers*, (a 1971 "community-history project; . . . sponsored by the Miles City Range Rider Reps, an auxiliary of Range Riders, Inc." according to the Montana Historical Society Library), Carrie briefly referred to Smokey's early life:

"Smoky [sic] had come up the trail from Texas with a cattle herd when he was only 14. His home had been on the Smoky river and from that he gained his name. He was much impressed by the lush valleys of western [sic] [eastern] Montana and by the size of the saddle horses, having been used to the smaller

---

* A relative suggested that brands "were probably recorded in his wife's name to avoid some brush he had with the law." (M.M.N. letter, February 3, 1981)

mustangs of the Southwest. He remained in Montana, living around the Ekalake area" (p. 364).

Mrs. Margaret Nichols recalled that the "family lived in Nebraska on the Smokey River — some time after Smokey left home Grandpa William Nichols and his wife and what kids were still at home walked out of their Nebraska place and moved to California."

Also in *Fanning the Embers* we learn that "Earl William Nichols, known to old timers by his nickname 'Bub,' was born at Fallon, Montana, in 1896. He was the oldest son of Anna Egan Nichols and E. W. 'Smokey' Nichols. Bub spent his entire life after he was six years old with his father, Smokey Nichols, on the Nichols' Ranch, first at the Dry House ranch on Dry House Creek and later at the ranch on North Sunday Creek. From the time he was a small boy he went on the roundups with his father and other men and worked with the horses on the ranch from the time he was big enough to rope and ride, halter breaking and breaking to the saddle the horses his father raised" (p. 309).

From the aforementioned documents, these facts emerge: Upon becoming a Montana resident as a teenager in the 1880s, Smokey was occupied with ranching on the Yellowstone River's "south side" around Ekalaka and Fallon, then by 1904 on the "north side's" Dry House Creek, finally establishing the UY horse and cattle ranch on North Sunday Creek in 1910, where he remained for the rest of his life. For unknown reasons, his brand was recorded in his wife's name sometime between their marriage in 1894 and 1910.

The foregoing statements in *Fanning the Embers* were clarified by Mrs. Margaret Nichols in letters to the author (June 24, 1982). In the letter, she wrote: "Smokey's original ranch was on unsurveyed land on Little Dry Creek, and there was also a Big Dry Creek which was swallowed up by the Fort Peck Dam. . . ."

On July 7, 1982, she wrote to explain Smokey's Inventory and Appraisement, which stated that ". . . in the matter of the estate of Earl W. Nichols, deceased" under the heading of Real Estate, the Sunday Creek ranch was described as "containing 320 acres more or less, according to the United States Government Survey. . . ." According to Mrs. Nichols, "When the government started to survey what was then Dawson County, Smokey moved to Sunday Creek in 1910. The creek was live, running water and he may have bought out someone who had proved up on a piece of land right on the creek and homesteaded on 320 acres, and bought out several other unhappy homesteaders because he had 1000 or more, possibly 2000 acres under fence."

Carrie had mentioned Smokey's "leased range," and Smokey in a court case testimony also referred to "leased range" which did not correspond with the ranch's size in the Inventory and Appraisement. However, along with other former ranchers interviewed by the writer, Mrs. Nichols pointed out: "Most ranchers did not boast about how much land or anything else they had to pay taxes on." She called attention to the size of several big corrals (as shown in pictures reprinted in this text), and "there were three large fenced pastures, all but one with running water." Undoubtedly, Smokey had to buy or lease more than 320 acres to support his horse and cattle stock.

Apparently Smokey's first marriage was not a happy one, for the Complaint dated October 15, 1907, charged defendant Anna Nichols with wilful desertion and abandonment since April 1906. Smokey, as plaintiff, petitioned for the custody of their four minor children: Earl William, a son, 11; Saul F., a son, 9; Nora, a daughter, 7; and Bessie, a daughter, 4. The plaintiff further "prayed" that the "bonds of matrimony . . . be dissolved." The District Court Minutes, November Term, 1907, noted that the case came for trial before the Court "without a Jury, default of defendant" and had been "duly entered herein November 27, 1907." Although the plaintiff was present with his attorney, the defendant was neither present nor represented. On January 15, 1908, the Court granted "the plaintiff, Earl W. Nichols a Judgment and decree of divorce from the defendant, Anna Nichols upon the ground of Wilful desertion, and awards

Chapter 6 — The UY's Colorful Boss

Smokey's original ranch house on Little Dry Creek (north of the UY Ranch on North Sunday Creek), on unsurveyed land, was built of sandstone slabs with very thick walls. "In winter," Mrs. Margaret Nichols recalled, "people left the livestock to shift for themselves and moved into Miles City or Fallon until spring. I was there once when I was quite young." (Courtesy, Mrs. Margaret Mann Nichols.)

the custody of the minor children, Earl Nichols and Nora Nichols to the plaintiff, and the minor children Bessie Nichols and Saul Nichols to the defendant. Decree signed and filed."

The couple's oldest daughter-in-law (Bub's wife) added these revealing and human interest sidelights: "I knew and liked Anna Egan Nichols who came from the large Irish Egan Family. It would have been better for all of them if the marriage had lasted. She helped him get his start, helped him gather wild horses, riding horseback with a side saddle."

While living on Little Dry, Bub told his wife that his mother, Anna, made shoes for the four kids out of cowhide, sewing the footgear by hand (Letter, July 22, 1982).

However, Smokey's ex-wife failed to release Nora to her father's care and custody, so on June 29, 1911, Smokey applied for and received a Writ of Habeas Corpus for Nora, his minor child, in which the District Court judge of Custer County commanded Anna Nichols to bring Nora before him in the courtroom on July 5, 1911.

Although Carrie did not mention Smokey's daughters when the writer interviewed her in 1934, she did refer to them in *Fanning the Embers*: the two girls Honora and Bess "attended the Convent in Miles City but were home in summer. Nora would play the piano and we would dance on the big screen porch." (The "convent" would be the Ursuline Sisters' Catholic Convent.) Nora's sister-in-law Margaret Nichols disputed "the bit about Nora playing the piano for them to dance on the porch" as "a laugh. Nora was never fond of music and could neither sing or play a musical instrument. The porch was about wide enough for one person to do a solo jig" (Letter, February 3, 1981). Two witnesses' recollections in a legal action seldom totally agree in all particulars, and this facet of human psychology holds true for all our memories of the past.

In addition to his domestic problems, Smokey spent some time in District Court as a defendant in four trials. The cases support Smokey's reputation for getting involved in assault actions and lawsuits resulting from his ranching operations. The first one was filed in the Seventh Judicial District for the term on May 20, 1901, and summarized in the District Court Minutes. Smokey and his brother Saul L. Nichols were charged with second degree assault. The brothers' case was set for trial June 4, 1901, and continued to September 26 after they were arraigned, and Judge Charles H. Loud fixed bail at $750 for each defendant. On September 28, the twelve jurymen informed the Court that it was impossible for them to arrive at a verdict. The judge then scheduled the case for retrial on December 13, 1901. The jurors announced their verdict on December 18 through their foreman, Dan C. McKay: "We, the Jury in the above entitled case, find the defendants not guilty."

The *Yellowstone Daily Journal* (Miles City, May 21, 1901) amplified the causes for the trial. The brothers were originally charged with grand larceny, accused of burning brands over a score of "Birdbread" cattle, and for being accessory to the crime of assisting Bill Clark, one of McPeak's gang of outlaws, to escape from a law enforcement officer. This charge was subsequently altered to first degree assault. But because the evidence was not deemed strong enough to convict them of this crime, the county attorney reduced the indictment to second degree assault.

The trial of Soloman [sic] and Earl (Smokey) Nichols held on December 16, 1901, was for preventing an officer from discharging his duties and second degree assault "with and without a revolver." The defendants then resided on Cedar Creek, where they assisted Bill Clark to escape from Emmett Wynne of Wibaux, who went to the Nichols ranch knowing Clark had taken refuge there, and the Nichols brothers supposedly "seized Wynne at revolver point and made him desist in his efforts." Sheriff John W. Goodall testified, however, that he had arrested the Nichols boys without difficulty.

Smokey's next brush with the law came on July 26, 1907, in the form of a complaint issued for Plaintiff Mrs. Erna B. Warren, who charged Defendant E. W. Nichols with the illegal possession of certain personal property, to wit: a gray horse valued at $100; a bay mare worth $75; a $65 Mitchell wagon; a $40 hay wagon; and a $20 set of harness — for a total value of $300.

The complaint continued in legal jargon: "That on or about the 23rd day of July, 1907, the defendant came to the tent where plaintiff was temporarily living near the Yellowstone Bridge on the Fort Keogh Reservation and told plaintiff that her husband, Lee Warren, had deserted her and gone to parts unknown, and then while plaintiff was laboring under great worry, distress and mental suffering and wholly incapacitated for attending to her business affairs, defendant alleged to plaintiff that her husband was greatly indebted to himself and others, and defendant further and falsely and fraudulently represented to plaintiff that he and other creditors, upon learning of the departure of her husband, would seize all of plaintiff's property to pay their claims against plaintiff's husband, and that it would save plaintiff trouble, annoyance and inconvenience if she would simply deliver to him her property so that it might be applied on his and other claims against her husband; that defendant by fraud, misrepresentation and undue influence, by fraudulently taking advantage of plaintiff's incapacity, procured her to agree to convey and deliver to defendant the greater part of plaintiff's property, including all of the above described personal property; that afterwards on the 24th day of July, 1907, plaintiff conveyed and delivered to defendant said property; that plaintiff owed defendant nothing; that defendant paid plaintiff nothing . . . that the said personal property had not been taken for a tax, assessment or fine pursuant to statute or seized under an execution or an attachment against the property of plaintiff."

Mrs. Warren demanded judgment for the "recovery and possession" of her personal property, "or the sum of Three Hundred ($300) Dollars" and one-hundred dollars damages and all costs of suit. However, some matters were alleged "on information and belief, and as to those matters she believes it [sic] to be true."

Written in ink on the last page of the Complaint appeared this

Chapter 6 — The UY's Colorful Boss

notation: "Dismissed as settled on Pltf's [Plaintiff's] Motion Wed — January 22 — 1908."*

It may be recalled that Smokey was also in court on January 15, 1908, for his divorce from Anna Egan Nichols. Other court cases in which Smokey was a defendant came about several years later, and these will be recounted in chronological sequence.

However, the old newspapers of the second decade of the 20th century, examined page by page by the writer, confirmed that urban and rural violence were not isolated or uncommon circumstances for the time or place. Smokey's tangles with the law were not exceptions. The papers reported a gamut of murders, assaults, burglaries, robbery, forgery, embezzlement, fraud, a few rapes, incest, grand and petty larceny, and rustling in communities and rural sections of central and eastern Montana. A theft case involved Smokey's neighbor, Denny M. Smith, who was arrested in August 1917 on a grand larceny charge of stealing three cows and three calves belonging to L. (or I.) Errick and William Errick, both the Miles City *Independent* and *Star* noted. Denny was held in lieu of $750 bail for trial in District Court for rustling in the "Stone Shack" country, a post office on Grimes Creek near its confluence with North Sunday Creek.

It was an era of change on the eastern Montana rangeland. As boy and man, Smokey had seen cattle ranching from the days of the unfenced free grass range to the coming of barbed wire

---

* *A letter from Margaret Reid, Deputy Clerk, Custer County District Court, to writer, September 26, 1980, stated: "File No. 2150 Warren vs Nichols, provides absolutely no information other than what I sent you previously" (May 9, 1980). Thus, details of the settlement remain unknown to the writer. When questioned about the case, Bruce Mott stated in a letter to the writer (October 20, 1981): "I am not familiar with the Warren-Nichols dispute. I knew Lee Warren in later years when he served as sheriff of Powder River County. He was married a second time then. I didn't know the first Mrs. Warren although she lived in Miles City near the old ball park. She had two children, a boy and girl. I remember going to school with them around 1910 or 1911."*

along with the arrival of hordes of "nesters" or homesteaders. The theft of cattle or horses had always been a problem, and it remained one in the new century. To curb rustling, cattlemen had organized the Montana Stockgrowers' Association in 1885, at the peak of the cattle boom, and hired seven detective inspectors to record brands while patrolling the range. One large operator in central Montana, Thomas C. Power, hired Pinkerton men from the famed National Detective Agency in Washington, D. C., for stock detective work.

By 1909 the Homestead Act had been changed to allow 320 acres rather than the original 160. Thereafter, dry-land farmers flocked in to the central and eastern parts of the state. They plowed up the native grasses to plant crops. Some homesteaders also raised sheep and they caused many confrontations with other stockmen, although never any large-scale "wars" as occurred in Johnson County, Wyoming. To the UY Ranch boss, the "woollies" acted like the proverbial red flag to a bull, a challenge to be met head-on.

Chapter 7

Carrie's Wedding and Rangeland Violence 1913

Spring comes suddenly to the range, Carrie reflected as she sa beside Smokey, jolting northwest along North Sunday Creek. During the first warm days of March, the snow had melted to patches on the shaded side of draws and hollows, and the grass had turned green. April had been cold and windy, but birds came to build summer nests and the first flowers bloomed. Green blades of grama-grass and blue joint had shot up in the swales, until now, in late May, they were nearly a foot high. Before she realized it summer began crowding in. Already wild roses had burst into full blossom along the creek. Sage hens and meadowlarks had begun hatching their eggs on a lush range that promised great things for the stockmen's future.

But different things for her future, Carrie reminded herself, because she and Smokey were now man and wife. The loveliness of spring on the range reminded her of the season when she and Bill had planned their marriage. At thought of him her throat constricted.

How differently her wedding had turned out compared to

what she had planned just a year ago! "Smoky [sic] and I," Carrie wrote in *Fanning the Embers*, "were married in 1913 at my home in Wisconsin and came back to his ranch to live."

The Miles City *Independent* (May 23, 1913, p. 5) reported: "'Smoky' [sic] Nichols and wife have returned from the east. Mrs. Nichols is a young lady who has been for some time a resident of the north side country in the vicinity of Mr. Nichols' ranch."

The spring roundup had started, which hastened the newlyweds' return. During the drive, the open parasol that Carrie held protected her from the sun's rays, but not from the smell of leather and sweating horses. Smokey, "brushed and shining" in a dark suit and white shirt, seemed like a stranger. But both ends of him were ranch country — his Stetson and his high heeled riding boots were the only familiar things about him. He reached up with one hand to loosen his starched collar and tie.

When Smokey had proposed, Carrie had put him off until the school term closed. She still clung to a fading hope that before then she would hear from Bill. Smokey's proposal had flattered her though. She had accepted him, a little voice deep within accused her, partly in a spirit of defiance aimed at Bill, and Sadie, too. Even though her fiance had jilted her, another man wanted to make her his wife.

As she stared at the landscape, she tried to console herself with the realities: Smokey was an established rancher, whereas Bill was a penniless boy whose ambitions and dreams of owning a grazing claim might never be realized.

Around her and Smokey grass-covered knolls dotted by sage and prickly pear cactus stretched northwestward. Eastward rose red, scoria hills. Clay cutbanks and coulees gashed the prairie, marking the tortuous course of dry stream beds. When she caught Smokey watching her askance, she swallowed her resentment at fate's doings and smiled at him. He rewarded her with a flash of white teeth beneath his mustache.

She squeezed his arm in a gush of affection for all his kindness and consideration these months past. Were it not for

Chapter 7 — Carrie's Wedding and Rangeland Violence

his comforting companionship, where would she be now? Growing into a bitter, old-maid schoolteacher because of a blighted romance? She banished the thought, resolving never to be lonely and heartbroken again.

After a silence lasting nearly a mile, except for the muffled "plupping" of the horses' hooves in the dust, the rattle of the wagon and the jingle of harness, Smokey asked tenderly what his little wife was thinking about.

"Oh, springtime, and how happy I am that I can look at the Smith place now without a shudder."

The rig was jolting past the house, barn, and sheds of unpainted weatherbeaten boards, looking more dilapidated and dismal than the year before. Carrie had never been within speaking distance of Sadie since she moved to the Dixons' following the showdown there. Walter Dixon had taken her to the Smith place in the sleigh and made idle conversation with Sadie while Carrie packed her suitcases. Sadie grumbled, but offered no active opposition. For the rest of the week, though, Minnie and Maria had been absent from school.

Only after Carrie had written a note to Sadie, threatening to report her to the school board for contributing to their truancy, had the girls reappeared. The oldest Arneberg boys, Carl and Eric, delivered the note and reported that Sadie did a lot of blustering and "cussin'," but that was all. After she had had time to cool off, she was smart enough to know when she was licked.

True to his promise, Smokey had sent a cowboy to act as Carrie's bodyguard during school hours and to convey her to the Dixons' afterwards. Walter always accompanied her and Norma to school in the mornings. As the ranch work grew heavier with spring's coming, making it inconvenient for UY hands to perform their guard chore, Carrie managed to convince Smokey that Carl and Eric were old enough and husky enough to protect her from Sadie.

Smokey turned the horses off the Jordan road into wheel tracks that wound through sage to the UY Ranch. Carrie described it as "a new ranch location so there were no chickens, no dogs, no cow or garden, only one old black cat (called Snowball) for company. I didn't even know how to cook, especially with canned milk and the limited assortment of canned goods available in those days. But the sourdough jar was there and I soon learned to use it." Apparently when she wrote that in 1971 in *Fanning the Embers* (p. 364), she had forgotten about helping sister Elsie with the cooking at the Griffith homestead and at High-Pockets Titus' sheep ranch in 1912. To paraphrase Shakespeare, "memory doth play tricks upon us all."

Smokey's granddaughter Nora described the ranch to the writer from her childhood memory: "The ranch buildings consisted of a two-room house with a porch and a small kitchen, a bunk house for the cowboys, a barn and an out-house [privy] used by all. . . . Life was not romantic or glamorous but in reality was hard work under the most primitive conditions" (Letter from Mrs. Nora Nichols Randolph, August 7, 1980).

Carrie's account in *Fanning the Embers* continued: "There were no radios or telephones, of course, but the stage from Miles City to Jordan passed the ranch and left mail once a week. Later on it came twice a week and, if necessary, I could go into town by stage. The stage was horse-drawn as an automobile was very seldom seen in our part of the country. In a very few years the Model T Fords began to become a part of the ranch scene" (p. 364).

While Smokey opened and shut the ranch gate, Carrie mused about her new estate. Here, as the boss' wife of the UY Ranch, she would find the security that her teaching job lacked, and as mistress in her own home she would enjoy the freedom denied her under her domineering father's roof. Secret elation filled her, too, because she, youngest of ten brothers and sisters, had a comfortably-off spouse, and so in a single stroke she acquired property, position, and prestige, outstripping the status of her senior siblings. She hoped she would find happiness here, too.

A week after Carrie and Smokey arrived home, range violence erupted at the roundup, a front page story in the Miles City *Independent* reported on May 30, 1913. Trouble long smoldering on the north side reached an anticipated climax "on Youall Creek in a fenced lane between two pastures." Sam "Goo" Roberts had been under suspicion by his neighbors. Goo was especially suspected of having "robbed Ray Lowe's ranch of about $87 worth of groceries, and when he [Roberts] and his wife made their appearance with the roundup. . . they were told that their presence was not desired." This incident occurred "on the horse roundup which started at Smoky [sic] Nichols' place May 15. The Nichols ranch is about 40 miles north of Miles City and the place where the shooting took place is about 40 miles distant from there, the difference representing the distance traveled by the roundup between the 15th and the 22nd." This mileage may refer to Smokey's former ranch on Dry House Creek, as the UY on North Sunday Creek was said to be 13 or 14 miles north of Milestown. It will be recalled that the bridal couple did not arrive at the UY from Wisconsin until May 22.

Roberts had left the roundup at the Nichols ranch, saying he'd be back again. "When the roundup reached Guy Truscott's ranch he and his wife came back, both armed" and made their camp "within about 50 yards of the roundup." On May 20, Goo warned Dr. Boyd who "was holding the saddle horses on a hill some distance from the roundup," that he intended to join the roundup to get his horses.

"I've got something here to protect myself with," he said, and patted his Winchester.

Late that afternoon, the camp was moved eight miles from the Truscott ranch to Youall Creek where Goo and his wife again set up their camp near the roundup crew's. The drovers were startled about 4:30 p.m. when Bub, Smokey's 17-year-old son, loped into camp, shouting, "Ray Lowe's shot; Goo Roberts shot him."

The "boys at camp jumped on their horses" and galloped to the shooting scene a mile away in a lane. Here they learned the

Earl William "Bub" Nichols, Smokey's elder son. Snapshot taken in Miles City by Bub's future wife, Miss Margaret Mann, when he was 17 years old. (Courtesy, Range Rider Reps President and Executive Board, from *Fanning the Embers*.)

Chapter 7 — Carrie's Wedding and Rangeland Violence

details. "A young fellow named Bill Lockey"* and Ray Lowe "were driving a bunch of horses through the lane" when Goo tried to stop Ray. "Ray told Roberts to 'leave the horses alone.' Roberts commenced to abuse and threaten Lowe and started to draw his gun. Lowe beat him to it and drew a gun from the saddle scabbard. Roberts then put his gun away and Lowe put his back into the scabbard, and then Roberts rode directly up to him, pulled his gun again and shot Ray twice through the shoulders and body."

Surprisingly, Lowe drove the horses about a half mile beyond the lane before he collapsed and fell from the saddle. Roberts followed him onto the flat, leaving his wife to warn away members of the roundup crew. But Goo permitted Dr. Boyd to approach and advise him to surrender. "After considerable parleying Goo consented," whereupon the doctor took a 30-30 Winchester and .44 revolver from Goo and a .38 from his wife.

"Roberts was then securely bound . . . hand and foot . . . and tied to the seat of Ralph Gilmore's truck." Dr. Boyd, Dr. McIntire, and Hi Gilmore piled into the truck and rode back to pick up the wounded Ray Lowe who was laid in the vehicle's rear. "When Smoky [sic] Nichols' place was reached, he also got aboard, standing on the footboard."

Mrs. Roberts was sent to her home, while "the boys cut out the Roberts' horses from the herd and helped her to get started towards her ranch."**

Meanwhile, the Gilmore truck reached Milestown at 1:30 a.m., May 30, where Lowe was taken to the hospital and

---

* *Probably Bill Lockie whose parents, James and Christina Lockie, emigrated from Scotland and bought a ranch on the Yellowstone near the mouth of Little Porcupine Creek where the Flying Y brand marked their horses and cattle after they gave up sheep raising. Bill and his five brothers (Dave, George, James Jr., Dan, and John) sold their combined Lockie Bros. 204,000-acre cattle ranch to Bruce Norris of Chicago in 1959 (**Fanning the Embers**, 249-251).*

** *Walter Mann added some specific details to the Lowe-Roberts assault case: "As I heard the Goo Roberts deal, Roberts came to the wagon on the*

Roberts to jail. Ray Lowe recovered from his gunshot wounds, and four years later, November 29, 1917, the *Independent* reported that he succumbed to head injuries from an apparent fall from a horse on his ranch. The Miles City *Daily Star* noted that Ray Lowe, 26, died in the hospital on November 23, 1917. The Miles City *American and Stockgrowers Journal* (November 29, 1917) stated that "George" Roberts "was tried at Glendive and acquitted on the ground of self-defense."

Here a long gap in Carrie's reminiscences had to be supplemented by contemporary newspaper accounts about ranching operations. After the shooting affair, ranch work returned to its usual routine — for a time. When the spring horse and calf roundup was over, Smokey and Bub rode away from the ranch early every morning to look after the welfare of the horses, check on the condition of pregnant mares, examine and treat any injured or sick animals, repair pasture fences, and size up forage quality before a hay crew arrived in July to help put up blue-joint and alfalfa for winter feed. Salt was scattered for horses and cattle. UY cowhands mainly attended to doctoring the cows and calves, and pulling out any unwary "critters" that got mired in bogs of mud or sand caused by the spring runoff in coulee creeks.

In late October, stockmen drove the beef cattle — steers and barren cows — to the railroad in Miles City for shipment to Chicago or Omaha stockyards for slaughter. It was not always a carefree occasion. The cowboys would encounter heavy rains

---

north side where Ray Lowe was wagon boss. Roberts had a mare in his string of saddle horses which is an out and out no, no in a cow camp. They wrangled over the subject and Roberts shot Roy Lowe, very serious, but he finally recoverd. Incidentally in later years, Ray had a horse called Black Hawk, very fast, which he rode in a quick change saddle relay race at Miles City. The saddle turned and he fell and broke his arm. Later Ray roped a steer on the north side range, his horse was jerked down, and Ray was killed. Ray's widow was working in the Ingham [Ingram?] Hotel in Miles City in 1965" (Letter to author, November 14, 1981). Ray Lowe, it may be recalled, adopted Tuffy Arneberg.

Chapter 7 — Carrie's Wedding and Rangeland Violence

which turned the dirt roads into quagmires, sometimes followed by a fall blizzard. Sleet and slush would then delay for several days delivery of the herd to the shipping point, where cattle cars would be sidetracked waiting.

During Carrie's early UY years, there were other typical stockraising hazards common to all eastern Montana ranchers and homesteaders. Cattle had to be treated for "blackleg" disease and dipped for ticks. Wolves attacked very young colts and calves; rabid coyotes would bite a number of animals, leaving them to die a painful death of hydrophobia. One year a quarantine prohibited the importation into Custer County of all domestic farm animals, including hogs, in order to guard the local stock against the dreaded "hoof-and-mouth" disease. Indeed, hundreds of cattle were destroyed in Montana to prevent its spread, resulting in a $40,000 loss, according to figures issued by the State Veterinary Surgeon (Miles City *American*, December 3, 1914). " 'Sheep measles' were found to be of common occurrence in the United States," the *American* had warned on October 2, 1913. On June 11, 1914, the same newspaper estimated that the Sunday Creek pens sheared 120,000 sheep in that area alone, a significant comment on the state's important mutton and wool industry.

Mrs. Margaret Nichols recalled: "There were huge bands of sheep on the north side of the Yellowstone River. When I lived at Fort Keogh as a small child, and the only bridge over the Yellowstone River in that area was through the Reservation, I have seen huge wagons after shearing season, sometimes more than one wagon loaded with wool pulled by as many as 20 horses, coming into the wool house on the Northern Pacific Railroad, the wool shipped by rail to the eastern states" (Letter, July 22, 1982).

Horse breeders also had their problems. Congressman Tom Stout secured enactment of a bill appropriating $100,000 for use in preventing the "devastating disease of dourine among horses," especially in the eastern range counties. "If allowed to spread this infectious disease of a horse's genitals and hind legs could mean the destruction of thousands of Montana's 380,000 head of horses . . . and a loss to the farmers and ranchmen of millions of dollars" (*American*, March 5, 1914, p. 3).

However, the country folk enjoyed good times, too. One example was the annual Stockgrowers' Convention in April, when horsemen, cattlemen, and sheepmen gathered in Miles City to work out their various problems, political and economic. Dancing and banquets enlivened the meetings. The July 4 Roundup furnished thrills and spills and other entertainment as cowboys and cowgirls competed in bucking, roping, steer bulldogging, and racing events.

At these rodeos, Bub Nichols distinguished himself. "Bub started doing a man's work as a boy and early carried the responsibility expected of a grown man. His education was in country schools and often the school year was of short duration but he was intelligent and learned easily and well."

"At the first Miles City Roundup in 1914,* Bub took part in the events — relay race, endurance races, Roman standing races, bronc riding — and was never out of the money." The *Independent* noted that Bub Nichols took first prize in the saddle bucking contest at the July Roundup in 1918.

"He was well on his way to becoming a successful rancher and had accumulated his own horses and cattle by the time he was 18 years old" in 1914 (*Fanning the Embers*, p. 309). Bub's initiative as an enterprising young stock raiser, fine horseman, and rodeo contestant was the more remarkable because he did not always enjoy robust good health.

Dancing, of course, was a favorite reason for gathering and socializing among the far-flung neighbors. The *Independent* reported that the O. N. Parker family held open house at their place on South Sunday Creek in 1917. All ranchers and homesteaders living on both South and North Sunday Creeks were invited to partake of the Parkers' large-scale hospitality. Games,

---

* *Newspapers stated the first Roundup was held in 1913, but the 1914 affair promised to be bigger and better.*

Chapter 7 — Carrie's Wedding and Rangeland Violence

Bub Nichols riding "Luny Jack" at Miles City Roundup, July 4, 1918, where he took first prize in the saddle bucking contest. (Courtesy, Mrs. Margaret Mann Nichols.)

music, and dances entertained 150 guests, the newspaper estimated.

Most of the time, Carrie was left alone at the ranch house, where isolation caused her to feel like a "broomtail filly" separated from the rest of the bunch and pastured with gentle work horses. As a bride she recalled: "I had been alone about two weeks when one of the neighbors drove in excitedly and said, 'You will have to come; my wife is going to have the baby. I'm going after Mrs. Dixon. I've saddled your horse. Hurry!' Nothing in my experience qualified me for duties as a midwife but, of course, I went along. I left a note saying where I was in case Smokey [sic] came home. Mr. Handley* was hardly out of sight when the baby arrived. I did as Mrs. Handley told me and by the time Mr. Handley and Mrs. Dixon arrived there was another boy in the house. I was glad to turn the situation over to Mrs. Dixon and was outside leaning against the corner of the house looking pretty pale when Smokey rode in. He leaned over with a big grin and said, 'Hi, Doc,' a nickname that stuck for some time" *(Fanning the Embers,* p. 364).

Such emergencies were not unusual in the lives of stockmen and homesteaders and were often the cause of human tragedies, as Carrie soon learned.

Fortunately, the winter of 1913-1914 was very mild with little snow, so livestock fared well. Running streams provided the only water for them when water holes froze up as happened when a cold spell came in February. Probably, the mild weather stimulated a mass migration of people. The Miles City *Ameri-*

---

* *Mrs. Margaret Nichols identified Robert Handley as Smokey's homesteader, farmer-neighbor whose land adjoined Smokey's north pasture on North Sunday Creek. Smokey "used Bob Handley's place for holding horses as his land was all fenced. Handley worked off and on for Smokey" (Letter to writer, August 31, 1981). Robert Handley was a retired farmer living in Clinton, Montana, in August 1982, according to Pat Cole, great-grandson of Smokey's brother, Sol. L. Nichols. Besides "a state job in Montana," Mr. Cole also has a farm at Clinton (Letter to Mrs. Margaret Nichols from Pat Cole, August 26, 1982).*

can (March 25, 1914) reported that there were an "exceptionally large number of emigrants pouring into the state with their goods and chattels, the Milwaukee [Railway] being exceptionally busy bringing in the new settlers who are locating all along the line from Baker to the upper Musselshell [River in central Montana]. . . . The greater portion of the movement is from the Dakotas, where partial crop failure last year led enterprising farmers to look for new locations . . . to secure lands in fertile Montana."

It was a foreshadowing of the future, which would prove mixed blessings in a few years for the new residents and for the state's economy.

Chapter 8

Plight of the Nesters 1914-1915

Carrie's compassion for sick animals — she already had a dozen sheep in the the calf pasture, raised on baby bottles from broken-legged or otherwise crippled lambs brought to her by sheepherders friendly with Smokey — extended to homesteaders generally, because of the hardships and utter isolation that were a daily part of their lives. Even at best she knew their lot to be a grim, cruel struggle to wrest a bare living from this untamed country. The spring, summer, and fall were subject to capricious weather changes and the winters were often long and cold.

Some years earlier the federal government had opened millions of acres of rangeland for settlement, and railroads offered low rates to prospective homeseekers. From the East and Middle West people of all ages, nationalities, and stations in life flocked to the plains of eastern Montana, thirsty for free soil. Attractive brochures pictured the range as a land suitable for growing grain and fruit trees and truck gardens, but neglected to mention the scanty, uncertain rainfall and lack of irrigation or that the natural grassland had nourished the buffalo and pronghorn antelope for centuries.

It became a pathetic sight to see former urban people and immigrants — Slavs and Swedes — futilely trying to make their acres or quarter-sections of rocky alkaline soil produce a wheat crop or potatoes or apples. The enlarged Homestead Act passed by Congress in 1909 had expanded the acreage per homesteader from 160 to 320. Then in 1912 legislation reduced the proving-up time from five years to three, and permitted an absence of five months each year. By 1909 over a million acres of land had been filed on for homesteading.

Even so, many gave up their barren attempts and returned to their old homes, disillusioned and penniless. Despite the failure of "square pegs in round holes," thousands of other hopefuls flowed into the state. The Miles City *American* (September 16, 1915, p. 5) noted "there were 20,827 homestead entries made in Montana in 1915, and over 19,000,000 acres of land still available to entry," according to the Federal Commissioner of Agriculture. The 640-acre Homestead Bill passed by Congress, December 30, 1916, and confirmed in the Miles City *Star* on that same date, would attract new rural homeseekers who "filed on homesteads close to Miles City," stated the *Star* (April 14, 1917), and proudly added that nearly 8,000 filings since July 1916 at the city Land Office had broken all official records of the West. Indeed, the *Star* (December 29, 1916) commented that one-fourth of all land homesteaded in the West had been "filed on in Montana."

A few of the more important early birds, realizing the unadaptability of the land to dry farming, turned their energies to raising sheep or cattle or both and succeeded in a small way. Of course, sheep breeding led to friction with the cattlemen, and monstrous was the latter's contempt for the "nester." Many older ranchers, like Smokey, had come up the trail from Texas, acquired free range, married, and settled down. Cattlemen were determined to keep the range open for their growing sons and daughters, of whom a goodly number were students at the state university. No actual warfare with the homesteaders had re-

Chapter 8 — Plight of the Nesters

sulted, but a state of hostile neutrality often existed on both sides.

Most of the poorer foreign nesters lived on the badlands' edge and some of them, Carrie well knew, were inexcusably shiftless, like the "Hunky" or "Honyocker" (Central European) family east of the Jordan road. After snow got deep in winter they could dig the lignite coal outcrops lying near ground surface on coulee sides or cutbanks, but the parents were too lazy to exert themselves and preferred to freeze when their scant wood supply gave out.

Out of sympathy for their youngsters, Carrie helped them all in any way she could — by gifts of old clothing or foodstuffs from stores in the ranch kitchen and "meat house." Discretion taught her to keep most of her charity from Smokey's knowledge because of his attitude toward nesters in general. Her kindheartedness earned her a reputation throughout the country, and whenever a neighbor, even thirty miles away, needed help, she was called upon.

Never would Carrie forget one winter on the ranch, owing to a series of harrowing experiences with weather and nesters and to the altercations they triggered with Smokey. Much of Carrie's oral history was vague as to dates, names, and places. Probably, the more unusual or dramatic episodes of her personal experiences were longest remembered. The two incidents narrated may have happened in 1915 or 1916. Smokey and the boys were away from the home ranch on the fall beef roundup in November after branding the summer crop of calves and foals.

Carrie recalled: "I was left alone at the house with a black-and-white shepherd dog named Shep, a maltese cat, and a black-and-white cat that loved to ride horseback, preferring Smokey's brown Music to any other horse. These animals I considered my best friends, and each one had its individual place in my affections. For a while I enjoyed the solitude of the quiet house with my animal companions."

Mounted on a filly that Smokey had given her, she rode the line fence every day to see that no wires were down and to keep a lookout for weak or sick cattle and horses. All female stock had already been herded onto winter range in the meadows, and calves and foals corralled where haystacks were available.

Riding homeward over the brown prairie in early twilight one afternoon, Carrie slapped her stiff hands on her thighs. The still air had become rapidly colder, and leaden clouds glowered low overhead. To restore circulation she urged the pony into a trot. She recognized the signs of a coming blizzard, and wouldn't have been surprised to see a violent late autumn storm hit the range before morning. Occasionally a storm swooped southward out of Hudson Bay and drove the mercury down to zero in a few hours, bringing with it a fine, hard, dry snow that cut the face like ice particles.

"While I was washing the supper dishes by lamplight," she said, "a blast of wind whipped out of the north and shook the house. In a few minutes it rose to a howl. I pressed my face against the windowpane and saw hard snow pellets being driven in swirls by the wind. How warm and cozy the kitchen felt, with the kettle simmering over a steady fire.

"The dishes finished, I dragged a rocking chair by the stove and settled myself for the evening. The maltese cat curled up in my lap and, purring, went to sleep while I studied the clothes and household furnishings in a mail-order catalogue. In my imagination I picked out the things I'd like to order. Shep and the other cat companionably shared the warm space between stove and wall."

The storm's fury increased during the night, the gale rising to shrieking banshee wails, and buffeting the house with an impact like a giant's sledge-hammer blows. Carrie slept fitfully, drawn into a shivering ball to keep warm.

In the morning she opened her eyes to snow drifts in the yard outside the bedroom window. After building up the kitchen fire and dressing quickly in freezing air that numbed to the bone, she stepped out on the back porch to read the thermometer. It recorded 15 below zero. The wind pelted her face with stinging snow missiles. She wrapped up more warmly and made the rounds to pitch fresh hay to stock in the barn. Afterwards, she had nothing to do but eat and read, make her bed, sweep and dust, worry about Smokey, Bub, and the crew, and listen to the raging blizzard.

"All afternoon with snow falling and wind blowing in roaring gusts, I played Chinese solitaire on the kitchen table by the hour. Tiring of that, I tried to invent new kinds of card games. Outside the wind howled and snowflakes whirled in a crazy mass. The cats and Shep remained snug in the house. There was plenty of food and wood to ward off the subzero cold that even seeped indoors. Isolated by wind and a blanket of white, I felt loneliness like a protective covering surround me. When several days passed and I had no word from Smokey or Bub, my worries mounted. I hoped he and the boys were safely holed up in a line-camp."

Then came a morning when the storm's rage was replaced by a stillness and profound silence that rang in Carrie's ears. As she walked toward the barn to do the chores, with Shep frisking about, the hard-packed snow creaked dryly under her boot heels. So sharp was the cold that it bit into her lungs and caused her nostrils to seal up when she breathed. All around the ranch stretched the white blankness of plains and rolling hills dotted by clumps of sage in windswept spots. On the horizon, smoky blue clouds merged into light gray ones overhead. In the creek bottom, bare-branched cottonwoods and willow brush seemed to huddle among boulders swept clear of snow. Sunday Creek's course past corrals and barn had frozen into a solid mirror of ice with rocks, like tiny islands, thrust up here and there. Drifts had piled dune-like in all the hollows and against the windward side of haystacks and buildings.

Carrie stood gazing for awhile with appreciative eyes, thinking the wintry scene a coldly beautiful work of architecture designed by the Storm King. Yet it worried her, too. What had happened to Smokey and the crew — and the livestock?

"That afternoon, just as I finished lunch, I heard the welcome stamp of boots on the back porch. I rushed to the door, my face all set to greet my husband. Instead, an ashen-faced cowboy in a sourdough coat stood gravely staring at me."

In a strained voice he asked, "Where's Smokey?"

His manner filled Carrie with apprehension. "What's the matter?"

"Where's Smokey?"

"He's out on the roundup and I haven't heard from him." Becoming aware of the intensely cold air, she invited him to come in where it was warm and tell what had happened.

He gestured toward his horse. Then Carrie saw a little girl about five clinging to the saddle horn and gazing blankly before her.

"I'll bring the kid in." He still spoke in a strained tone.

Although mystified, Carrie remembered to call after him to turn his pony into the barn and fork it some hay.

When the child was settled with a bowl of hot canned milk and bread, and Carrie had given the cowboy a steaming cup of strong coffee, he beckoned her to a far corner of the kitchen.

In a low voice he explained that she belonged to "them Roosians near the badlands." He had taken a package of mail to their place and stopped in to get warm. There was something "plumb queer and empty 'bout the shack" as he walked in. "It was all freezin' cold inside, an' there was her ma layin' on the bed with her throat slit from ear to ear." The sight turned his stomach. Then he noticed "the kid jist sittin' nearby, dumb-actin' like she is now, an' near frozen."

Carrie gasped in horror, her scalp prickling. She looked at the child's thin, pinched face, her dirty dress and matted, wheat-colored hair. Having eaten her fill, she sat tapping the spoon against the rim of the bowl, and showed no interest in her surroundings.

He explained that he couldn't tell how long the mother had been dead, and there was nothing to show who did it. So he picked up "the kid and high-tailed it out of there." He thought maybe she could stay with Carrie while Smokey got the sheriff.

Carrie bit her lip to stifle another gasp and shook her head in

Chapter 8 — Plight of the Nesters

pity. When she could trust her voice, she told him he'd better ride down to Miles and report the murder and the orphan child to the sheriff. She would look after "the poor little thing."

He agreed, and buttoning up his sourdough coat, went out into the frozen cold.

For a long while Carrie stared at the small girl, wondering what fiend could have committed such a crime, and for what motive, and why was the child's life spared? Or was it suicide? She never learned the answers to these questions, although suspicion pointed to the woman's husband, a drummer, who disappeared after his wife's death. The shock, however, added white hairs to Carrie's black ones. The author found no mention of the case in any of the Miles City newspapers, although all microfilms of them had pages missing.

At last, going over to the girl, Carrie asked her name, but received only a dumb stare. Then she picked up the maltese cat and showing it to the child began stroking the fur as she repeated, "Nice kitty. Don't you want to play with the kitty?" The child just continued to stare at her.

Carrie lowered the cat to its feet, and nonplussed, left the nester girl to amuse herself by monotonously tapping the spoon against the bowl. She washed the lunch dishes and swept the floor, brooding on life's stark cruelties on the range. From Western stories she had read back home, she used to imagine living in cattle country would be all romance and pleasant excitement. Now she deplored her childish ignorance.

Smokey and the boys rode into the ranch in late afternoon. Carrie heard the muffled thud of hoofbeats, but she was mixing bread dough and could not get her hands cleaned in time to greet them. Smokey hurried into the house and took her into his arms, apron, dough-covered hands and all. As he bent to kiss her, he noticed the strange little girl sitting on the floor between stove and window, beating two tin pans together. Drawing away from Carrie, he demanded, "Who's she?"

"Oh, the most terrible thing has happened!" Carrie exclaimed, and told him of the Slav woman's murder.

He listened with unchanged expression, and when she finished he called to the girl to "cut out that noise!"

The child stopped her clatter and stared vacantly at him. Then she resumed banging the pans together.

He declared he'd fix that, and going over to her grabbed the pans. The child just looked at him. He regarded her for several seconds, and then turned to Carrie, telling her she couldn't keep that "half-wit around here." She'd drive them all crazy.

"Only until the sheriff comes."

He ordered Carrie to have nothing to do with "them damn nesters." They were good for nothing but trouble.

Carrie turned to stare at her husband, her fingers again thrust into the sticky bread dough. She said they couldn't turn their backs on a helpless unfortunate like her.

"That kid belongs in the state orphanage," he growled, and told her to see that the sheriff took her soon as he came. He stamped out of the kitchen into the next room.

Carrie frowned at the doorway through which he had disappeared, taking an aura of coldness with him. A wave of dislike went through her. What a change from his charming manners before her marriage. Not that he had ceased to be the perfect lover when the mood aroused him, but she censured her own naivete for not seeing through the surface charm to the faults beneath.

Somewhat embarrassed, Carrie explained there were times when his tender love-making gratified her. Other occasions he frightened and repelled her. To a young woman reared under the Victorian code of manners and morals, conjugal sex was a necessary evil to be submitted to at the husband's whim and for his pleasure. The shy, repressed Carrie found her husband's amorous outbursts another harsh reality of life that engendered fears about her marriage.

He was right about the child, of course. The orphanage was the proper place for her. But it gave Carrie's heart a twinge when the sheriff and matron arrived in a sleigh to take the wretched little girl to Miles, still suffering traumatic shock. Carrie

Chapter 8 — Plight of the Nesters

determined to go on helping the nesters in spite of Smokey's disapproval.

Another opportunity came during the winter. Smokey was riding over the ranch to see how his stock were weathering and to doctor any sick or injured animals. Carrie had just taken several pans of golden brown bread out of the oven. While putting them to cool on a clean dish towel spread over the table's oilcloth, she heard a knock at the kitchen door.

She called to the visitor to come in and recognized the thickset form of a Hunky [Slovakian] nester from over on the badlands. His uncut black hair straggled about the collar of his sourdough coat, and the offensive odor of an unwashed body clung to him. Dried horse manure stained his heavy overshoes.

Carrie restrained a desire to hold her nose and said sociably, "Hello, Ike. How's the wife and kids?"

He pulled off his cap and mumbled through unkempt black whiskers, "That's what I rid by to tell. My ole woman had 'nother baby last night." Hunger lit up his eyes as he stared at the fresh bread and smelled its appetizing aroma.

"*Another* baby? Why didn't you let me know beforehand? I might have been able to help." Carrie went on turning out the hot loaves.

He said he went to bed and the woman was lying beside him, and when he woke up this morning there was the baby in bed with them. "How'd I knowed she was goin' to have it durin' the night?"

Carrie no longer blushed at such matters, and hastened to ask how the mother was feeling.

So-so, but he wished she could "coom over an' kinda look after t'ings a bit. Cood yuh?" He ran his tongue around his bearded lips.

"Why, certainly, Ike." After telling him to go out to the meathouse and pick out some steer beef, she changed into riding clothes and fixed up a couple loaves of fresh bread and some potatoes.

His black eyes had shone in gratitude as he thanked her and

shuffled outside.

She tucked a large jar of buffaloberry jelly into the pack of food. Carrying it to the barn, she saddled the filly and stowed the bundles in the saddlebags. Ike tied the piece of meat to his own dilapidated saddle and the two of them set out for his shanty.

A pale sun peered through gray clouds. Occasionally the ponies floundered through deep snow while crossing the coulees on the way to the sod dugout, which faced south on the creek bank about ten feet above the stream. No smoke was coming from the stovepipe that stuck through an inverted lard bucket. Ike led the horses into the stable. It had been dug out of the cutbank and the front pieced together with scrap lumber, slab rock, railroad ties, and tin cans.

Her arms loaded with food, Carrie shouldered aside the sheepskin covering the doorway and stepped into the hovel's dark interior. She stood blinking a few seconds to adjust her eyes to the dimness and shivered in the clammy cold temperature inside. A variety of stale odors almost nauseated her. She couldn't hear a sound until one of the children coughed and the newborn baby uttered an animal-like whimper.

Gradually the dugout's earthen walls, dirt floor, homemade wooden table and chairs, bench, and washbasin took visible shape. At the far end she made out a double bunk and pallets on the floor where the children slept. On dirty — incredibly dirty — blankets the woman lay in the lower bunk, the baby nestled beside her asleep. Carrie noted the mother's dull, brutish features and long, stringy hair, unbraided and unkempt. Four other children, the youngest scarcely able to walk and suffering apparently from malnutrition and rickets, watched Carrie out of hunger-haunted eyes as she laid the food parcels on the table. The mother spoke no word of greeting but observed her with an impersonal stare as Carrie shook down the cold ashes in the four-hole, wood-burning stove. Evidently no fire had been lighted for hours.

When Ike came in, Carrie told him to chop some wood, or dig

Chapter 8 — Plight of the Nesters

some coal, so she could get a fire started right away. He mumbled something and went grudgingly out.

What a hovel to house human beings, Carrie was thinking, as she went over to inspect the cupboard. In cowboy idiom their "grubstake was down to a whisper," for she was able to find only a bit of old black bread.

After Ike got the fire going, she brewed a coffeepot of the tea she had brought along, warmed the milk and put potatoes on to boil. Then she sponged the baby and tidied up the woman. To appease the hunger of all, she had sliced a loaf of bread and spread jelly thickly on the large-sized pieces. The children ravenously wolfed it down, but the mother gave Carrie and the fresh, wholesome food a withering look.

Turning her face to the wall, she said flatly, "Black bread's goot 'nuff fur me!"

Nonplussed and somewhat chagrined, Carrie stared at her. For once she was ready to agree with Smokey's opinion of the "sodbustin' nesters." Slowly, though, she perceived that the woman's proud disdain of her poverty caused her to act as she did.

"All right," Carrie said cheerfully, "if you prefer it," then told Ike who had put some meat on to stew, that she'd better be starting back. It would soon be time to get supper ready.

Mounted on the filly, she rode homeward on the snow-covered trail. She drew in long breaths of clean, cold air, thankful to be rid of the stench in the Hunky dugout.

Back at the ranch while she was unsaddling in the gathering blue twilight, Smokey rode in.

Eyeing the empty saddlebags, he demanded, "Where y'all been?"

She explained that Ike's wife had a new baby last night and she went to straighten things up. It was pretty tough for her with four other kids and that shiftless husband. She hoped the explanation would satisfy him, as he seemed already out of sorts.

"And I s'pose yuh took a lot of grub along. Or," he inquired with polite sarcasm, "did yuh leave enough for our supper?"

"There wasn't a speck of food in that dugout," Carrie retorted with a flash of spirit. "You can't let them starve."

Smokey snapped, "Hell's fire, let the county take care of 'em. I cain't afford to support all the damn nesters."

That set off another controversy as Carrie attempted to defend the hard lot of the homesteaders. When, as usual in their married life, neither party would yield to the other's views, each accused the other of being at fault. After the spat, a self-pitying mood of disappointment in the man she had married depressed her. She probably didn't realize that she, too, had changed, grown more self-assertive, even aggressive, in expressing her opinion.

Carrie never mentioned the following incident, which revealed a different aspect of her husband's complex nature. The Miles City *American* (August 12, 1915, p. 1) reported the event, headlined "Honyocker Gets Off Easy."

"A nester just over Custer County line in Rosebud County upon finding a horse trespassing on his property, shot and killed the animal which belonged to E. W. (Smoky) [sic] Nichols. The horse was then hauled to a well and dumped in and the well filled up in an effort to cover up the heinous deed. But Smoky was on the job a few days later, and after the honyocker had denied all knowledge of the horse's whereabouts, he (Smoky) started to dig out the recently filled in well. At this stage of the game the suspected one coughed up all he knew — which was plenty to send him over the trail to the tune of ten years [in prison]." Because the honyocker had a family "in anything but flush circumstances" Smokey made a settlement for the horse's death: a bill of sale for a cow to cover the loss of his horse:

"I hereby give Smoky Nichols one cow unbranded, to settle for horse found in my well."

Signed _____

"This fellow . . . can thank his lucky stars that he got out of it so easily."

The killing of the horse was a felony, the item noted,

"punishable upon conviction of not less than one nor more than ten years imprisonment in state Prison." The paper did not identify the nester by name, nor his place of residence.

Chapter 9

A Lonely, Youthful Wayfarer 1914-1916

Wayfarers, according to the country custom, were always dropping in at the UY Ranch, sometimes to stay for a meal and not infrequently to spend the night. Some were drifters who "rode the grub-line," going from ranch to ranch and living upon the hospitality of the cowboys until their welcome wore out. So, on that bright, sunny noonday, Carrie was not surprised to see a lad with a darkly tanned complexion come striding toward the kitchen porch. His horse stood a ways from the house, head drooped and reins hanging to the ground. Holding several sticks of wood in her arms, she awaited the youngster's approach.

The boy smiled as he asked in a diffident voice if there was "any chance to get work around here." One hand caressed Shep's muzzle as the dog wagged his bushy tail.

Carrie's eyes widened in astonishment. The boy didn't look more than thirteen or fourteen years old. Carrie smiled back and said he seemed rather young to be looking for work. " How old are you?"

"I'm fifteen," he replied brightly.

"Oh." When she asked his name, he hesitated, and then answered slowly that they called him Saul.

She had been studying him and guessed that he wished to conceal his identity for some reason. In her friendliest schoolteacher manner, she told him to turn his horse in the corral and fork him some hay, then to come in and have a bite of lunch with her. After they'd eaten they could talk about jobs.

When he came to the table, Carrie noticed he had used the tin wash basin and comb at the bunkhouse. His hands and face were clean and his hair neatly combed. His handsome features had an oddly familiar look that nagged at her memory. As she set a bowl of steaming gravy and a platter of boiled beef and potatoes before him, she remarked chattily that her husband and the boys were out rounding up horses to break for the sales, so she was glad to have company for lunch.

Inside the kitchen the air was hot. Despite the heat, though, the savory odors of freshly cooked food whetted the appetite — especially the boy's. Only a fitful breeze stirred through the opened windows and screen door, on which several flies buzzed hungrily.

Carrie pushed a pitcher of milk close, inviting Saul to help himself and not to be bashful. She sat across the table, wiped the perspiration from her face, and led the conversation along general lines as she helped herself to the food. From his remarks she learned that he was familiar with the country, and knew a great deal about Smokey and the UY Ranch. After she had served him a quarter slice of dried apricot pie, she put the question she had been burning to ask, "So you want a job, but haven't you any parents? Or are they dead?"

He squirmed in his chair and admitted reluctantly that his dad and mother were divorced.

She realized that her next question would violate the unwritten code of the cattle country where every man and woman was taken at face value, but she said casually, "By the way, who is your father?"

He twisted again and a flush spread over his tanned face. Eyes on his plate, he mumbled, "Smokey's my dad."

"Oh!" Staring at him she made hasty calculations. She had

Chapter 9 — A Lonely, Youthful Wayfarer 109

Saul Francis "Dutch" Nichols, Smokey's younger son, on his buckskin pinto pony. Picture taken in Miles City, Montana, in 1919. Saul would be 21 years old. He is on a Rafter T horse. (Courtesy, Walter E. Mann.)

been married over a year, so Smokey's younger son, whom she had never seen, would be fourteen or so. "Then you must be Dutch!" she exclaimed. At his sheepish nod, she assured him that of course he could have a job. His job would be to live with his dad and her and go to school.

He met her eyes squarely then, the lonesome light in his kindled by pleasure. "Gee," he grinned, "I never thought you'd be like this!"

Carrie smiled in answer to the implication of his words. It was understandable that he, a child of a broken marriage, longed to join his father and older brother on the ranch, since country life was more attractive to him than town life.

This was essentially the story Carrie told the writer during interviews in 1934. In 1971, though, she gave a different version to Walter E. Mann, who had gone to "grade school in Miles City with Nora, Bess and Saul." Mr. Mann was the son of Michael F. and Rosa B. Mann. His father, a sergeant-major in the 22nd Infantry, was stationed at Fort Keogh, where Walter was born in 1900. Walter Edward Mann is now a retired administrative officer of the U.S. Forest Service living in Ogden, Utah, where he had been employed in the Intermountain Forest and Range Experiment Station. His sister Margaret later married Bub.

In a letter to the writer (October 28, 1981), Walter Mann recalled that "Carrie was at the ranch in 1918 when I worked on the north side. She came here to Ogden twice to see me about 10 years ago. She lived in Chico, California, and was failing fast. She told me Saul came to the South [sic] Sunday Creek ranch in 1914 and stayed overnight. She did not know him. As he was getting on his horse the next morning, he said to Smokey, 'Good-bye, Dad.' Carrie said, 'Is that your son?' Smokey, 'Yes.' Carrie, 'Why don't we make a home for him?' So Saul returned and lived there and worked for Smokey to the end — about 1919" [actually 1921].

Mr. Mann's sister Margaret told essentially the same account about Dutch which her husband Bub related to her: "Late one night a couple of men and a very young boy stopped at the ranch and were settled in the bunkhouse. There Smokey and Bub had a conference with young Sol [sic], and the three decided Sol should stay with them. The two boys were delighted to be together and Smokey was happy to have his younger son. This matter of Sol staying at the ranch was settled in the bunkhouse and Carrie had to be hoodwinked into believing it was her idea to take him in" (Letters to writer, August 16, 1982 and August 31, 1982).

Carrie intimated to the writer that Dutch's arrival triggered a family argument with Smokey over his younger son's education.

However, in later years, Dutch's wife Esther told their daughter Betty Grayce that her father had graduated from high school in Miles City. That would be about 1916. Dutch's (Saul's) Death Certificate gives his birthdate as August 15, 1898. Thus, it is presumed that he spent summers on the ranch and winters in town attending high school.

Domestic disputes with her husband and other unpleasant memories, like the case of the Russian nester child and the Hunky family childbirth incident, had begun to plague Carrie. But not a word of her marital unhappiness had she written home to her mother or other relatives, nor to sister Elsie. Her pride wouldn't let her.

Because of the proliferation of sheep raising in eastern Montana, Carrie witnessed another incident, of far graver personal importance than the preceding nester episodes. When she told her experience to the writer in 1934, Carrie was again vague about pinpointing the date, place, and name of the person, and the case did not surface in any of the Miles City newspapers or the District Court records.* Thus it will be narrated as an unverified reminiscence of Carrie's that may have taken place in May or June of 1916.

One of Smokey's outriders galloped to the house one night to report that "his sidekick at the line-camp got shot by a damned nester," after the cowboy told the man to move his sheep off UY range. Apparently the herder ignored the order, so the puncher shot at a few "woollies" to show he meant business. Provoked, the sheepherder shot the cowboy in the back. He made it to the linecamp and told his partner, who rode posthaste to the home ranch.

Line-camps were usually built of cottonwood logs, located at the edge of an outfit's range as temporary shelters for outriders.

---

* *In a letter to the author, September 16, 1980, Deputy District Court Clerk Mrs. Reid wrote about this incident: "I could find nothing anywhere that would show your pistol-whipping of a John Doe. My only thought is that perhaps it never got any farther than justice court."*

THE LINE CAMP. "This snug log cabin was a permanent camp for these two cowboys caring for the cattle on their portion of the range perhaps a day's ride from ranch headquarters." Could be typical of the one where Pat Loney, Smokey's outrider, took refuge after being shot by a trespassing sheepherder on UY range. (Courtesy, Coffrin's Old West Gallery, Miles City, from L. A. Huffman photo.)

Chapter 9 — A Lonely, Youthful Wayfarer

They patrolled the ranch borders to turn back other ranchers' cattle or sheep that drifted in winter storms or were allowed to trespass on another man's property.

As he rode away with the outrider, Smokey told Carrie not to worry, he'd be back soon.

Carrie could understand Smokey's vexation with sheepowning homesteaders under ordinary circumstances, but one who had "plugged" a UY puncher in the back would, she knew, anger him mightily. He had told her why cattlemen were the natural enemies of sheepmen. Unlike cattle, sheep ruined grass because they cropped it to the roots. Consequently, cattle and horses starved on land where sheep had grazed. Most of the UY spread was grassland reserved for cattle and horses. They were Smokey's pride and joy.

But knowing these things did not lessen her fears. "What a night of apprehension for me," Carrie related. "In my restless sleep I visioned my husband shot to death in a gun battle."

At the first gray tinge of dawn she left the much-tossed bed and made a pretense of cooking and eating breakfast. Every few seconds she ran outside to search the prairie for a dust cloud that might signal Smokey's return. She forced her mind to concentrate on realities around her to lessen the tension, noting the sunlight and shadow on cottonwood trees and willow brush along Sunday Creek near the barn. A breeze stirred the leaves into a gentle rustle.

Beyond the hills eastward lay barren stretches of badlands. Bands of wild antelope lived among them.... It was no use. Her eyes insistently moved back to the range.

"Late in the morning while I was cleaning the house, Smokey rode in with his prisoner whose hands were tied behind him. Smokey's casual greeting helped to soothe my tense nerves. He stayed long enough to gulp a hearty breakfast, and then departed for Miles to put the nester in jail, there to await trial for first degree assault.

"He was a little man in dirty, patched overalls. I saw livid bruises on his hard-featured face. One eye was swollen and the other appeared glassy and shifty, probably still dazed from shock. He had avoided looking at me in sullen silence and had refused to eat. A blood-soaked, blue bandana handkerchief had been wrapped about his head and partly covered by a battered, dusty, black sombrero."

The sight made Carrie feel queasy. Smokey explained that the herder put up a fight and had to be subdued by slugging him on the head with the barrel of his six-gun. She could imagine the beating the nester had received. Had Sadie, then, been right in warning her against Smokey? Sadie had told her of his reputation and quick temper. Doubts began to nag at her.

For weeks Carrie was unable to shut the memory of the nester out of her mind. Smokey made no further reference to the matter, except to assure her that the outrider was recovering in the hospital.* But the chain of circumstances resulting from this episode, and other of life's harsh realities on the range for which her sheltered girlhood in Wisconsin had not prepared her, made Carrie's black hairs turn white. When she learned that the nester had become insane and was taken to the asylum in Warm Springs, she wondered whether the beating Smokey had given him was partly responsible. The incident shed new light on his temper.

---

* *Don R. Pyle, a former cowboy from the "South side," told the author in a telephone interview, September 29, 1981, that Pat Loney was Smokey's outrider in the line-camp on the east side of North Sunday Creek who was shot by a locoed sheepman. Mr. Pyle, 84, is a resident of Miles City who spends the winter with his wife in Phoenix, Arizona. Bruce T. Mott, another rancher who knew Smokey, "was not familiar with the Pat Loney incident and did not know Loney personally. I remember his name as the owner of a bucking horse name 'Sky Rocket' that was quite noted in this area" (Letter to the author, October 20, 1981).*

Chapter 10

Mystery of Bill Solved 1916

Elsie had been writing Carrie urging her to come over to the homestead for a visit. The two had not seen one another since Carrie had left to teach. When Smokey and the boys rode away to round up and break horses for foreign army buyers, Carrie accepted the invitation. Elsie was throwing a party to celebrate Junior's coming birthday. It would be near his sister's second, so she wouldn't "take 'thank you but can't' for an answer this year." A lot of the neighbors were invited for a good time and George would meet Carrie at Westmore.

A change might do her good, Carrie decided, and give her a new perspective on her marriage. She refused to let herself think about the fact that Sis' place held romantic memories of Bill. She had put him out of her life and would no longer permit his memory to disturb her thoughts. But she had often wondered how she would react if she ever saw him again, and whether or not he had changed in almost four years since she had last seen him. He would now be twenty-two. Only once in Sis' letters, after Carrie's marriage, had she mentioned him. Billy hoped Carrie would be happy, she had written.

Cowboys operating hand-powered ranch "laundry." DeLoss McBride on left, Dutch on right wearing chaps. (Courtesy, Mrs. Margaret Mann Nichols.)

An older, more weather-roughened George met the train with the spring wagon, but he was his same old even-tempered self. His eyes had become squinted to mere slits from years of gazing far distances on the prairie. Innumerable crow's-feet radiating from his eyes gave him an amiable rather than a sinister expression. Outside of asking how Carrie was "gittin' along over on Sunday Crick," he did not pry into her affairs, but willingly answered all her questions about Sis, his growing family, the homestead, the prospects for the crops, and the stock. Bill was not mentioned, nor was Smokey by name.

Once George asked how many horses "was the UY runnin' now?"

Carrie thought around three- or four-hundred or so. George

Chapter 10 — Mystery of Bill Solved

whistled, as she explained they had a few cattle, but it was mostly a horse outfit.

He shook his head, saying, "My gosh! That's a *lot* of stock."

She continued that Smokey sold young, sound geldings to army buyers for foreign cavalry and artillery use in the European war. They were buying hundreds of horses a week, for over a hundred dollars each, from ranchers all over. And some of the horses went to Fort Keogh for the Remount Service. Old horses and barren mares Smokey disposed of to farmers and homesteaders. He had mares with foals, and coming three- and four-year-old geldings. He was rounding them up for the British and French governments. But he was building up his beef herd.

Upon arrival at the homestead shack, Carrie found Sis heavier, but otherwise little changed. Perhaps her plain features had become more weather-beaten, but her hair, which she still braided and coiled around her head, remained the same brown. Junior had his father's strong type of face, and his sister favored her mother. The greatest change Carrie noticed was a large bedroom added to the shack, and a partition dividing the large original room into a kitchen and dining-living quarters. She saw no sign of Bill, nor did she inquire about him.

Carrie's whitening hair amazed and shocked her older sister, who asked if her marriage was unhappy. It wasn't the marriage, Carrie told her offhandedly, it was the stark brutalities of life she'd seen in this country, and reminded Sis how sheltered they had been at home.

For several days she enjoyed the visit with Sis and Peggy, the girl who had become Worden Vandervoort's wife. Peggy was a round-faced blonde, full of natural good humor. Once during their conversation, Sis remarked that Billy "took up a homestead," then she went on talking about how many cattle George was running now with a few sheep. Carrie was aware of the measuring look Peggy gave her and thought it odd. A queer tingling at the sound of Bill's name agitated Carrie, although outwardly she managed to remain composed. It was her first intimation of Bill's whereabouts. She had presumed that he was either still working for George or on a neighboring ranch.

On party day, homesteaders and their wives and children began arriving early in buggies, in wagons, on horseback, and in a Ford car or two. Carrie and Peggy were up before dawn, helping Sis make enough sandwiches to fill a wash-tub it seemed, slice up quarts of pickles, and boil water for gallons of coffee.

During the days she had been at the homestead, Carrie observed that Sis never gave her and Peggy a chance to talk privately. Today the constant arrival of guests caused too much distraction for Sis to keep her eye on the girls every moment. Adult conversation hummed in the air, frequently shattered by children's shrill cries and the running patter of small feet indoors and out. Little knots of women stood or sat about the rooms, exchanging gossip and recipes. The menfolk and older boys, of course, congregated at the barn. Sis was hurrying thither and yon, chatting with first one neighbor, then another, and seeing to the general comfort of her guests. Midday heat and mellow sunlight diffused through open doors and windows.

The girls, by themselves, buttered slices of bread spread out on the kitchen table's oilcloth. Its fresh, yeasty, homemade odor, combined with the salty tang of newly-churned butter and the aroma of hot coffee, wafted an appetizing fragrance in the kitchen. With a side-glance at Sis' figure disappearing into another room, Peggy leaned close to Carrie and asked guardedly if she ever saw anything of Bill since her marriage.

"No," Carrie replied shortly, as she didn't want to reopen that painful subject. Mere mention of his name, though, caused her abdominal muscles to contract in an effort to quiet the excited trembling that shook her. But she could not still the rapid beating of her heart. To find herself getting all aflutter once more annoyed her.

Peggy eyed her shrewdly as she confided that Bill couldn't savvy why she never broke the engagement before she went off and married Smokey.

Dumbfounded, Carrie stared at her, the butter knive sus-

Chapter 10 — Mystery of Bill Solved

UY/Rafter T roundup chuckwagon with cook Carl Arneberg about 1917 or 1918. Carl was Tuffy's brother. Tuffy enlisted in the Navy at eighteen and retired as a Chief Petty Officer. Carl, Mrs. Margaret Nichols recalled, "left Montana for the West Coast and worked his way into the building industry and did very well. He and Tuffy often visted each other." (Courtesy, Mrs. Margaret Mann Nichols.)

pended in mid-air. "Why *I* never broke the engagement —," she echoed in confusion. "What about him? Why didn't he answer my letters?" she demanded, resentment and challenge in her voice. In self-defense she added that Sis kept writing her what a good time Bill was having — going to dances and such. She insinuated he'd lost interest in her. And he had never written her a line.

Peggy became wide-eyed in amazement.

Carrie explained she'd written him right up 'til Christmas in fact. But when he didn't reply —. A sob choked off her voice.

Peggy shook her head in bewilderment and declared he never got any letters. He told Worden that Elsie told him she was having too much fun — with other men — to care about a penniless cowpoke any more. Elsie said she'd set her cap for a wealthy old duck who owned a big spread. Bill was all broke up over her marriage, but Elsie seemed right pleased. Peggy added she was terribly sorry.

Tears had misted Carrie's eyes as the heartrending truth exploded in her mind — Sis had deliberately lied to Bill about her because she was jealous of him! Yet never once had she suspected Sis; she'd thought Bill's love had cooled to indifference. For some moments red and black specks ringed by scarlet danced before her eyes. An impulse to choke her double-dealing sister possessed her, followed by a fit of nervous trembling. She clenched her hands and bit her underlip. What a cruel, tragic mistake all her heartache over Bill had been. Why hadn't she swallowed her precious pride, made a personal investigation, and talked with Bill before she married Smokey? Why? Why? Self-recriminations kept pounding at her. Why hadn't she seen through Sis before? There had been many hints. Of what use now was the knowledge of Sis' duplicity? Out of the first shock she found a glimmer of solace: Bill hadn't jilted her. That knowledge raised her self-esteem.

Peggy stared in blank astonishment at the tears streaming down Carrie's face, at her white hands gripping the edge of the table. Uncomprehending, she asked what was the matter? What

Chapter 10 — Mystery of Bill Solved

did she say to upset Carrie? "Wasn't it true?" she added.

Carrie swayed backward and raising her hands pressed the palms over her eyes and forehead. She faintly excused herself to go outside.

Peggy suggested the root cellar; no one would disturb her there. She'd make up some excuse to Elsie.

Shortly after Carrie left the kitchen, Peggy told her later, Sis bustled over to the table and spoke excitedly to her, asking how were the girls making out? Would they have enough sandwiches, did she think?

Peggy assured her there were plenty, and blurted that Carrie was still crazy over Bill, wasn't she? And why had she married Smokey instead?

Peggy said Sis gave her a long, strange look, then said she didn't think so. She'd forgotten about him long ago. Where was she? Sis didn't wait for an answer but hurried over to the stove where a persistent hissing sounded from a pot of coffee boiling over.

Half an hour later, her composure recovered, Carrie peeped cautiously from the root cellar door. Groups of men loafed about the barn and corrals. Children ran in play into the coulee between house and stable. The women were all clustered in and about the house. Having made her reconnaissance, she walked rapidly down into the brush of the ravine and laved her eyes with the creek's cooling waters. Its purling flow soothed her, as did the breeze faintly stirring willow and alder leaves.

Outwardly calm, she reentered the kitchen and, going over to the table, listlessly began spreading jelly on the remaining sandwiches. Sis was outside at the pump, and being intent on her chore paid Carrie no attention.

Peggy stared at her dry, reddened eyes and inquired was she feeling better?

Carrie nodded, knowing that Peggy didn't realize how completely she had spilled the beans.

Peggy's kind tone expressed sympathy as she asked if Carrie wanted to tell her what was the matter, because maybe she could

The UY Ranch's impromptu "ambulance" for ailing Stock Inspector Font Hitchcock who had to leave the roundup in 1918 because of illness to get medical treatment in Miles City. Nurse Martha Hagerman is the "driver" who transported him from house to vehicle. (Photo by Mrs. Margaret Mann Nichols.)

help.

Carrie explained it was Sis. She'd lied about Bill and her to each other. And she must have read and destroyed their letters.

Holding two slices of bread in mid-air, Peggy gasped out her amazement. "She did? Why would she do that?"

Carrie shook her head, suggesting they not discuss it. But she

Chapter 10 — Mystery of Bill Solved

asked Peggy to tell her about Bill. Again quivering shook her.

After a pause, Peggy exclaimed she could hardly wait to tell Worden Elsie was the snake in the woodpile. Worden had always blamed Carrie. He thought she considered herself "too good for an ord'nary cowpoke."

Carrie grinned at Peggy, telling her to be sure to set her straight with Worden.

"Indeed, I will. Yes, indeedy, I will," Peggy promised. Carrie repeated her question about Bill.

Peggy related that after Elsie told them all she'd married Smokey, Bill went about all that summer "like a locoed bronc," Worden told her. He had helped George with the roundup and haying though. Along about November he told Worden he'd decided to drift to a new range; it might help him to forget Carrie.

The girls stacked the sandwiches and then began slicing up more dill pickles, releasing the sour odor of the relish while they talked in low, confidential tones.

Peggy continued after Sis came and went on various chores, giving the girls a wary glance each time. Bill had punched cattle until he turned twenty-one. Then he filed on a grazing claim.

Heads bent, they continued their task, while the ceaseless chatter in the house ebbed and flowed around them. Outside, children laughed, shouted, and uttered excited cries at their play. Junior was the envy of the kids in his spanking new cowboy suit from a Chicago mail-order house. Several times one of the visiting women strolled over and asked politely if she could help. Assured that she couldn't, each drifted back to the crowd.

Carrie's final question choked her up, but as she darted a watchful eye about for signs of Sis or other possible interruptions, she managed to ask whether Bill had married.

Peggy declared that the last time he wrote Worden he said he was off women. Carrie felt strangely relieved. Somehow she managed to get through that harrowing day. She had to restrain herself, though, from visibly shuddering every time she looked at her double-dealing sister, moving from group to group and chatting gaily. Some of the older women had settled down to do their mending or sewing after eating lunch.

Sis and Carrie slept late the next morning, though George rose early to attend to the never-ending ranch chores, and then rode off to repair fences. Carrie had made up her mind to say nothing to Sis about what she had learned. Sis would undoubtedly try to lie out of it, and accusations would only lead to harsh words. Better to quietly ease away from Sis' place. With that in mind she had arranged with Peggy to call for her after breakfast and drive her to Westmore where she could catch the train to Miles.

When the girls sat down to a late breakfast, Carrie casually remarked that she had to leave today. Then she commented that it was clouding up. The hazy air had a sultry oppressiveness, preceding later summer rains, probably. She felt dull, spiritless, with a let-down feeling after the noise, activity, and disclosures of yesterday. By contrast the shack seemed depressingly quiet and empty.

Sis looked searchingly at her, saying George wasn't here to take her to the train. Carrie informed her that Peggy would drive her to the station.

Sis demanded a reason for sudden leave-taking. Carrie offered the excuse that she didn't like to leave the ranch too long. She toyed with her food, the sickening sweet taste of which almost gagged her, miserable and depressed as she was. Breakfast cooking smells hovered in the kitchen, further nauseating her.

Was that the only reason, Sis shrewdly persisted. "Carrie, what's really eating you?"

Carrie studied her sister for several seconds. Then, pushing the half-eaten plate of pancakes away, she spoke bluntly on a sudden, rash impulse as a wave of hatred swept through her. Why, she shot back, had Sis lied to Bill about her? Why had she tried so hard to break them up — that spring and summer Carrie stayed with her? And what did she do with Carrie's letters to Bill — open and read them and burn them? Sis had asked for it, and

Chapter 10 — Mystery of Bill Solved

she got it with both barrels.

Sis' glance wavered and slowly a blush began to creep up her neck and spread over her face. At first she blustered, denying she had ever heard of such a silly thing, and what on earth was she talking about?

Carrie gazed fixedly at her sister. "Don't lie, because I *know* that you did."

Sis countered evasively by accusing the gossiping Peggy of telling wild tales behind her back, and she should have heard the way Peggy talked about her.

Hurt and angered beyond all caution, Carrie let her know her eyes had been opened at last. Was she in love with Bill? Was that why she'd acted like a dog in the manger about him? It was a pretty mean trick to play on her naive, trusting sister! Had her treachery brought her any happiness?

At first dumbfounded by her formerly shy and reserved kid sister's savage outburst, Sis heard her out, and then cried wildly that she couldn't talk to her like that! "You can't! You can't!" Hysterical sobs began shaking her. Her face fell forward into her open palms.

Carrie interpreted the emotional display as theatrics intended to woo sympathy and cloud the issue. Unmoved, she contemptuously watched Sis a few seconds. Rising from the table, she walked toward the bedroom to pack her suitcase. Pausing by the door, she advised Sis to enjoy her little act! She'd got her answer, and if she ever saw Bill she'd tell him the truth. What kind of opinion would he have of his sister-in-law then?

Sis became conciliatory, denying she meant any harm to Carrie, swearing she didn't! "You kids just didn't seem suited." Sis' protests came mumbled through a tear-broken voice. She thought she was saving her sister from an unhappy marriage, and reminded her she did make a better catch. Oh, couldn't she understand?

Carrie said bitterly she could understand Sis betrayed her. She turned on her heel and passed through the doorway out of the kitchen, annoyed to find herself trembling. The palms of her hands were coldly moist from nervous perspiration.

In the bedroom she packed hastily, stuffing clothes in with reckless disregard for wrinkles or neatness. When she returned to the kitchen, coat and hat on and suitcase in hand, Sis jumped up from the table and rushing over clutched her arm. She implored Carrie not to go off mad like that, but say she forgave her, 'cause she was truly sorry. She wouldn't do anything in the world to hurt her. She then invoked the childhood oath, "Cross my heart and hope to die!"

Still outraged, resentful, sorely hurt to the core of her being, Carrie roughly pulled away from Sis and left the house without speaking. She paused only to give a hug and kiss and a dime to each of the children who were playing outside. Then she trudged on with her weighty burden, almost endlessly it seemed, along the wheel tracks before sitting down on the suitcase to wait for Peggy's arrival with the spring wagon. Nearly exhausted, she was breathing heavily and perspiring from exercise and emotion. Glancing back she saw the children still standing near the kitchen porch and waving tiny arms at her. Sis slouched forlornly against the doorjamb.

With a twinge of regret, Carrie turned away and stared at the twin, dusty ruts of the road ahead, flanked by clumps of buffalo grass and sage. Now that the showdown was over, she felt ashamed of her melodramatic leave-taking. Things had turned out so differently from what she had planned. More deeply than the betrayal, the loss of a sisterly friendship distressed her. Well, what's done is done, as Shakespeare said, and there was nothing she could do about it.

Moist, still air pressed against her skin, but inside she began to feel a joyful release from the burden of doubt about Bill. A film of dust over the tawny, rolling hills rose against the cloudy sky and indicated that Peggy was coming. Carrie decided to give her a goodwill message for Bill, informing him of her sister's duplicity. She wanted him to know that she hadn't "sold her saddle" in the cowboy lingo for a double-cross. It would be many years before the breach with Sis was healed.

Chapter 11

An Elopement and More Violent Crises 1916-1917

Several events happened before and after Carrie's emotionally traumatic visit with sister Elsie, so she had little time to dwell on the unhappy disclosures Peggy had made. A brief local item in the Miles City *American* (July 13, 1916) announced to the young friends of Bub and his steady girl that E. W. Nichols, Jr., and Miss Margaret Mann were married at Glendive. "The couple will reside on the groom's ranch on the north side." (Bub had filed on 320 fenced acres.) The bride, a daughter of Mr. and Mrs. Michael F. Mann, was born at Fort Keogh where her father became caretaker after the garrison's abandonment as a military post. In later years she added to the news statement: "I attended Custer County High School and when I left there, I obtained a job in the post office in Miles City — $50 a month for ten hours a day — and I was on my way to fame and fortune.

"On July 7, 1916, Earl (Bub) Nichols and I eloped to Glendive. Although Bub had $700 he had won at the Miles City Roundup, we were both apprehensive of the reaction of our families and we hurried home to Miles City. I was welcomed

Margaret Mann Nichols, Bub's widow, taken in "the Mesilla Valley at Las Cruces, New Mexico about 1927." (Courtesy, range Rider Reps President and Executive Board, from *Fanning the Embers.*)

into the Nichols family by Bub's father, Smokey, and his young stepmother, Carrie. In April, 1918, our daughter, Honora was born" *(Fanning the Embers*, p. 310).

Carrie, the "young stepmother," was two years Bub's senior, so her relationship with the newlyweds was apparently more that of a younger brother and sister-in-law until later, when tensions developed. Curiously, Carrie said nothing about Bub's marriage or his activities to the writer.

Following the shooting of UY outrider Pat Loney by the transgressing sheepherder, Carrie related: "During that summer we were troubled by other small flocks of sheep belonging to nesters who let their animals graze on our range. Smokey had told me to order off any sheepherder I might find trespassing. One afternoon I was riding along a coulee when I noticed a flock of 'woollies' eagerly nibbling grass belonging to UY cattle and horses. Since my line of direction would take me right by them, I decided to caution the herder. He was a hard-featured young man, and when I told him his sheep were on leased range belonging to my husband he let fly a stream of oaths. I paid no more attention to him and rode on, feeling sure he would move his sheep.

"A few days later when Smokey returned to the ranch I told him about the incident, described the man, and suggested that the fellow would bear watching as he appeared shifty. Smokey said nothing to me, only nodded."

Here another gap occurred in Carrie's reminiscences. She never mentioned Smokey's various legal troubles.

The new crisis struck on September 29 when Smokey was charged in the Sixteenth Judicial District Court of Custer County with "assault in the second degree" upon one John McLean for inflicting "grievous bodily harm" with a "large .45 caliber Colt revolver or 'six-shooter,' which the defendant held in his hands and delivered three stout blows with it upon the head of said John McLean." Trial date was set for October 18.

Meanwhile, when McLean came to town to file his complaint on September 29, and to have his injuries dressed, he told a different version of the assault to the *Star* (September 30, 1916) than in his sworn testimony during the trial. The newspaper reported "he was camped near the Milwaukee stockyards and had a six-shooter lying on a bed, but that Nichols took his own gun and beat him over the head with it."

The *Star* on October 5 quoted McLean as having brought sheep into Miles City along with seven other sheep ranchers from the north side. Also on the same date, the paper (p. 5) reported great activity in the sheep market, with about 20,000 sheep "being in the course of shipment to points east or west and local dealers have been busy delivering and making new sales." Apparently, it was business as usual with John McLean, who had accused Smokey, in legal jargon, of "unlawfully, wilfully, wrongfully and feloniously" inflicting "grievous bodily harm upon him."

Six days later, Smokey's hearing for assault was continued to October 11, the *Star* explained, as his attorney Herrick was busy in a land office case, but Justice of the Peace John Gibb bound the defendant over to District Court on the assault charge.

During McLean's testimony at the trial, his replies evinced a surprising lack of understanding. County Attorney Frank Hunter's questioning brought out that McLean had been alone on the range herding sheep when he first saw Smokey Nichols and Denny Smith "going over on Krueger Creek with a bunch of cattle" where "they went out of sight in Krueger Creek," then reappeared riding towards him on horseback.

"How far north from Miles City, if you know?" asked Attorney Hunter.

"Well, it would be south by west, I think," was McLean's answer.

"About how far from Miles City?"

"Seven or eight miles, I guess."

"Do you know what county and state?"

"Well, it is in this county, I think."

"That would be Custer County?"

"Yes, sir."

"Montana?"

"I think so."

Continued questioning by the county attorney revealed factual details of the encounter, summarized here from photocopies of court records. On reaching McLean, the men dismounted and Smokey asked whose sheep they were. "I told him they were McLean's and my partner's John McKinzie." When Smokey accused him of being the man who had been less than a gentleman toward his wife "up on Sunday Creek," McLean denied it but said he "knew the party your wife was talking to." Smokey asked who they were and McLean answered, "I wasn't out for information but I happened to be going for the mail to the Stone Shack and happened to know that they had been talking to his wife and his wife had been talking to them. I ate dinner with them and they told me." McLean refused to divulge the man's name and Smokey insisted he was the man his wife told him she had talked to. McLean again denied it and explained that he was *lying on his right side* on the ground with "a gun" on his lap, which Smokey picked up declaring, "You are the party. My wife told me you were the man."

"Well, if your wife told you I was the man your wife was lying."

Smokey demanded, "Do you mean to call my wife a liar?"

"I said, 'No, I don't mean to call your wife a liar,' and that was about all there was to it when I got [h]it on the head."

After receiving three blows with a ".45 Colts," McLean testified that he was paralyzed, couldn't move, and "lay over on his right side" (after just testifying to being in the same position during the dispute). He was "bleeding pretty freely" on top of the left side of his head, and had difficulty talking, "could only get a few words" occasionally. Smokey cursed him and said, "The last time I saw you, you spoke like a gentleman."

When Smokey and Denny Smith offered to wash McLean's head in the creek, he told them to leave him alone. "I didn't want that creek water on an open wound in the condition the creek was in then. I didn't say that to Smokey. I said to leave me alone."

As is usual in court trials, certain details of the assault testified to by defendant Nichols differed from that of plaintiff

McLean. While looking for certain cattle, Smokey and his neighbor had chanced to meet McLean at the mouth of Krueger Creek. Smokey's testimony, also abridged here, follows:

"When we rode up to him I recognized him as a fellow I had been wanting to see for some time. I got off my horse and asked who he was herding for and he said he was herding for himself." McLean remembered a previous meeting with Smokey "up on Alkali sometime before in the summer." Smokey had asked if he "remembered talking to my wife and little girl one day and he said he didn't. I says 'I think you do.' "

Attorney Herrick asked, "This conversation that took place was relative to what?"

"Relative to herding on some leased land that I have. He said he didn't but he guessed he knew who I was talking about." The men then argued as to whether McLean was the culprit, his repeated denials, and refusal to tell Smokey the alleged offender's name. "I said from the way my wife described this man and from where your wagon was when I saw you, I am positive you are the man. He said if she said he was the man she lied and he raised up with the six shooter pointing right at me."

Herrick questioned: "At the time this conversation took place where was the man McLean?"

"He was sitting down on the ground." Smokey was standing to his left and Denny Smith was "behind more on the left. He was sitting down on kind of a raised place." Smokey declared he didn't know McLean had a gun, as he "didn't have on any belt." But when McLean pointed the weapon at Smokey, he "grabbed it" and a scuffle ensued. Smokey wrested the revolver away from McLean and "hit him with it. Denny stepped in kinder between us. The man fell and Denny picked him up, lifted him up and took his hat off and asked him to come to the creek and he would wash his head." But McLean said "he was all right, to let him alone."

When Smokey accused McLean of carrying the gun for him for some time, the sheepman declared he was afraid of a bull on the creek. Smokey said the bull was his and he didn't want it shot. Then McLean said he was carrying it for coyotes. So Smokey turned the gun over to Deputy Sheriff Al Truscott of Custer County the next day.

After the altercation, Smokey and Smith rode down the creek a short distance with a bunch of cattle and observed McLean "going around the sheep." The trouble took place "about five miles" from the UY Ranch where Smokey had "a couple of pieces leased."

Under cross-examination the county attorney was unable to shake Smokey's testimony. Following the fall term of District Court, the trial resumed on January 16, 1917. During the winter term Carrie and neighbor Denny Smith appeared as witnesses for the defense. (Apparently, friendly relations had been established between Mrs. Smith and her erstwhile teacher boarder, following the showdown.)

Not until March 17 was the case submitted to the jury. On that same day, according to the Court Minutes, the jury returned to the courtroom with their verdict: "We, the jury in this case, find the defendant not guilty. Dated this 17 day of March, A. D. 1917. C. N. Wynes, Foreman." The Court then ordered the defendant discharged.

On March 20, the Miles City *Star* reported: "E. W. Nichols (Smoky) [sic] who was on trial last week for assault, was found not guilty Saturday. Nichols was charged with beating up John McLean, a sheepherder, with a gun. The complaining witness, John McLean, was charged by the defense with having used abusive or worse language before the defendant's wife."

A year after Smokey's assault case, McLean got himself involved in another beating. On September 23, 1917, the *Star* reported:

> John B. McLean, sheepman, charged neighbor J. W. Reed, cattleman from the Jordan country, with brutally beating him. Reed is charged with second degree assault before Judge Welch. The pair met in Tom Jones place in Milestown, became involved in an argument which resulted in

Bub Nichols "going some" on Pat Loney's "Skyrocket" at Miles City Roundup. (Courtesy, Mrs. Margaret Mann Nichols.)

blows. Reed is alleged to have knocked McLean down, beat and kicked him when he was down. . . . McLean was found to be seriously injured. He was taken to the hospital. . . . In addition to many bruises . . . his ankle was found to be broken.

The case was taken under advisement and defendant Reed bound over to the District Court. The author found no further mention of the case in the newspaper. McLean's two known conflicts with cattlemen were typical of the antagonisms engendered by the proximity of the two kinds of stockmen competing for the range forage.

Former cattle rancher Bruce Mott recalls a sidelight on McLean's troubles: "I remember the Nichols-John B. McLean squabble. McLean was quite a prominent sheepman who was prone to partake of spirits occasionally, at which times he became a little feisty" (Letter to the author, October 20, 1981).

The sheep industry was well established in the state by 1917. Indeed, the *Star* (December 29, 1916) claimed that sheepraising was the most remunerative industry on the plains, with 35 cent wool prices predicted as a result of the great demand for woolen cloth by the warring European nations. By March 1, 1917, wool was selling at 40 cents a pound and had leaped to 60 cents in June. The *Star* (June 30, 1917) announced 700,000 pounds of wool had been shipped out of Miles City despite the severe winter and scarcity of feed. One enterprising rancher, Stanley Smith, even piloted his own plane to keep track of his sheep, his herders, and range conditions, according to the *Star* (January 7, 1917). If the 640-acre Homestead Law became operable, the *Star* warned (May 2, 1917), sheepmen would suffer greatly due to the drastic reduction in the amount of grazing land. When the act did become law, many large sheep ranchers sold off their stock. New homesteaders, though, carried on the business on a smaller scale.

The winter of 1916-1917 was very cold with much sub-zero weather and heavy snowfalls, and was said by old-timers to be one of the severest in 30 years. Meteorologists concurred in this record. Ranchers were obliged to ship in hay from Washington and Minnesota. Despite this they suffered an excessive winter kill among both cattle and sheep. As early as December 23, 1916, the *Star* described the difficulties of country travel by car when George Nichols and F. A. Shaffer drove 50 miles to town. "Between Crow Rock and Yuall [sic] Creek a saddle horse pulled them for two miles to help them to the main road, as snow was over the fenders."

Probably Carrie was referring to this same severe winter when she recalled: "One winter the snow was so heavy and deep that we had no mail for six weeks and reading material was nonexistent. I found my high school Ancient History and started to read it. The cowpunchers insisted I read it aloud and we finished Ancient History and part of Medieval by spring. The first question on reaching any ranch was always, 'What do you have to read?'

"Harry Hall loaned me *The Clansman* and I read it aloud three times in one week to the roundup crew who took turns coming in to hear it. When the movie was shown in Miles City as *The Birth of a Nation* we all rode in to see it" *(Fanning the Embers,* p. 365).

Dan Lockie, one of the six Scottish Lockie brothers who were cattle and horse ranchers on the Yellowstone River near Miles City, tells an incident about his range horse's remarkable intelligence which is also an unusual story of human survival. The spring of 1917, following his marriage to Blanche Hawley, then 21-year-old Dan recalls:

". . . We had a late spring storm and I went out to the head of Bull Creek to look through the pastures. I was riding a horse called Dewey that my Dad had given me as a colt and I had broke myself and wouldn't let anyone else ride. When I was gone for three days, Blanche began worrying and on the third morning said she awoke to Dewey's nickering. She wondered about it and pretty soon, from her kitchen window, she could dimly see the horse on a rise in the road, coming slowly along, jumping from

Chapter 11 — An Elopement and More Violent Crises

Saul "Dutch" Nichols on his UY-Rafter T horse, taken sometime prior to 1928, the year of his tragic death. (Courtesy, his daughter, Betty Grayce Nichols Kalfell.)

side to side. She and my mother went out to the gate and saw that I was on the horse, unconscious, with my hands frozen to the horn of the saddle. The horse had brought me home and had to find his way around three fenced homesteads. He was keeping me in the saddle by jumping sideways so I couldn't fall off. I can dimly remember becoming terrible sick and waking up enough to get out of bed and thinking, 'I have to get home.' I remember calling Dewey but don't remember putting the saddle on him or his bringing me home. As far as we can judge, I must have been sick in that bed for a day and a half, and it must have been late in the afternoon when I got on Dewey and he brought me home just at daylight the next morning. Blanche sent for her mother to nurse me through a bad bout of double pneumonia; I was still unconscious for three days after they got me home. But that faithful horse Dewey had saved my life.

"I've always thought a lot of the old horse; he was a man's best friend and he helped him pioneer this country" (*Fanning the Embers*, p. 247).

That same winter (1916-1917), a sensational murder trial made front-page headlines, along with European war news and rumors of America getting embroiled despite President Woodrow Wilson's efforts to remain neutral. Paul Schultz, a young drayman in Miles City, was found mysteriously murdered with a blunt instrument in his warehouse on Thanksgiving Day, November 30, 1916. Jack Logan, 21, who had been working on the Schultz north side homestead since March of 1916, and Mrs. Schultz, 24, later proved estranged from her husband, had been at the ranch that day. They were questioned by the sheriff but released for lack of evidence.

The case broke wide open, January 7, 1917, when Mrs. Paul Schultz and George Van Lanningham, alias "Jack Logan," were arrested in Kirksville, Missouri, where Mrs. Schultz had gone shortly after Paul's death to join boyfriend George, alias Jack. She accused him of killing her husband after George married his former hometown sweetheart, who had given birth to a bastard child. The jilted lover, Mrs. Schultz, became hysterical at the unexpected turn of affairs and signed an affidavit against George. He was convicted in Miles City and sentenced to life imprisonment in the Deer Lodge penitentiary. The *Star* noted in August 1917 that Van Lanningham asked for a new trial on the grounds of "new evidence" but the judge denied the motion.

After America's entrance into the Great War (April 6, 1917), to "make the world safe for democracy," wartime inflated prices affected animal feeds on both the north and south side of the Yellowstone River. Charles Daly, a Stacy farmer, told the Miles City *Independent* in August that he had sold his hay crop of 400 tons at the amazing price of $15 a ton, realizing $6,000 for it in the stack.

Farmers' picnics were held in mid-June as usual near Miles City. At these, J. E. Yerrington, acting county agricultural agent and brother of C. M. Yerrington, the county agent, and other prominent speakers encouraged farming to help the war effort. Baseball games, music, and dancing were the favorite entertainments of the day.

Meanwhile, more trouble was brewing in the summer for the Nichols family. On July 24, 1917, the *Star's* headlines and subheads dramatically announced: "SMOKY [sic] NICHOLS SHOT BY FARMER; Bullet Wound in Shoulder; Lays in Critical Condition at Hospital; Assailant Now in Jail; Bad Feeling Existed; Scores are Now Evened Up; J. [sic] W. Kraft admitted shooting.

"Sunday evening July 22, about 8 o'clock, a messenger came to Miles from the north side with information that Smoky [sic] Nichols, a well-known horseman, had been shot at his ranch, about 14 miles from Miles City, and two miles the other side of the 12-mile bridge.

"Deputy Sheriff [Al] Truscott and Dr. [W. W.] Andrus left immediately for the scene of the trouble followed by M. H. Wallace with the ambulance.

"They found Nichols with a bullet wound in his shoulder, made with a 30-30, the ball striking back of the right shoulder and lodging in the left. The wounded man was placed in the ambulance and Miles City was reached about two o'clock yesterday morning [July 23], Nichols standing the trip as well as could be expected. The story told the *Star* is about as follows: Nichols and his son Saul [Dutch], about six o'clock, took some cattle down the creek to a pasture and on the return when in a draw, were fired upon by J. [sic] E. [sic] Kraft, a homesteader near the Nichols ranch and between whom it is said bad blood existed.

"The Krafts will be remembered at the time of the Van Lanningham trial, when they were witnesses. Kraft came to town after the shooting Sunday night, gave himself up and is confined in jail pending the outcome of Nichols' wound, which, though painful, is not considered serious." The Miles City *Independent* reprinted the news story verbatim on July 27, 1917.

A former ranch hand of Smokey's remembered an incident when Smokey had befriended farmer Kraft the year before the shooting, after he complained to Smokey, "If you don't keep those cattle out of here, I'll shoot you." "In 1916 Smokey donated 5 rolls of barbed wire to homesteader Kraft whose place was about one mile SE from the 12-mile school house, to help keep range livestock out of his crop area. Saul [Dutch] and I hauled the wire to Kraft's homestead with a team and wagon. It is my recollection there was no one at home when we left the wire. Smokey and Saul were moving some cattle by the Kraft homestead in 1917 when Smokey was shot off his horse" (Walter Mann's letter to author, November 14, 1981).

A follow-up on Smokey's condition appeared in the *Star* on July 29, and in the *Independent* on August 3. Both papers reported that Smokey Nichols was gaining daily. He had been x-rayed, the bullet was located in the shoulder and removed. Kraft was still in county jail "in default of five thousand dollars bail."

Kraft's trial for first degree assault was scheduled for October 8, 1917, on the District Court docket before Judge O'Hern.

On August 3, the *Star* noted: "Smoky [sic] Nichols was down town yesterday for the first time since being shot at his ranch on the north side of J. [sic] W. Kraft."

It was an eventful year for both the Nichols and Denny Smith families. Through means unknown to the author, the Smiths' fortunes had improved to the point of affluence. The *Star* (October 3, 1917) announced that Mr. and Mrs. D. M. Smith had bought the Hyde Hotel in Miles City after A. Becker had purchased the new Smith ranch of 1600 acres. (The UY home ranch was officially only 320 acres, according to a court Inventory and Appraisement.) Becker brought a large number of Mexican cattle to Montana to stock the former Smith ranch. Other local news items in the *Star* told about Mrs. Smith making frequent trips to visit friends or relatives in the Midwest.

Among the Hyde Hotel's guests, the *Star* noted on October 28, 1917: "Mr. and Mrs. E. W. Nichols and Mr. and Mrs. Ray

Chapter 11 — An Elopement and More Violent Crises 141

Lowe of North Sunday were at the Hyde Friday. Messrs Nichols and Lowe made up a large shipment of cattle which they took to South S. Paul." It was the first time the author discovered mention of Carrie in the local news of any papers. The Nichols were mentioned again at the Hyde "while stopping in the city" on November 2, 1917, three weeks before Ray Lowe's death, November 23.

None of the papers gave any publicity to the Kraft trial until a hint appeared December 6, 1917, in the Miles City *American and Stockgrowers Journal* (p. 2): "Judge C. C. Hurley arrived for Glendive to hold court for one day" in order to clear up some of the accumulated cases during Judge O'Hern's lengthy illness, which had prevented his appearance on the bench. Hence it wasn't until March 21, 1918, that the same paper informed its readership:

> In the case of the State vs P. [sic] W. Kraft, who was charged with first degree assault, E. W. (Smokey) Nichols being the complaining witness, charging Kraft assaulted him with a gun last summer, the jury returned a verdict of second degree assault and fixed the penalty at from two to four years recommending a suspended sentence. The case against Mrs. Kraft, who was named as a co-defendant in the action, was dismissed.

Again it was the Custer County Court records, rather than the press, that supplied further details. The trial began on March 18, 1918. Although Odessa Kraft was arraigned as co-defendant with her husband, P. [sic] W. Kraft, the charge against her was dismissed March 19. The next day defendant Kraft learned the verdict.

John E. DeCarle, the foreman, announced: "We, the jury in the above entitled action, find the defendant P. W. Kraft guilty of Assault in the Second Degree as charged in the information and hereby fix his punishment at imprisonment in the State's Prison for not less than two years nor more than four years." The foreman added: "We, the jury in the above entitled action do respectfully recommend that the above sentence be suspended."

On March 21, Judge C. C. Hurley issued the Order suspending the sentence and stating ". . . it satisfactorily appearing to the court that the character of the defendant and the circumstances of the case are such that he is not likely again to engage in and [sic] offensive course of conduct and it appearing that the public safety does not demand or require that the defendant shall suffer the penalty imposed by law. . . . the said defendant shall be placed on probation under the control and management of the State Board of Prison Commissioners and subject to the rules and regulations of the same as applied to persons paroled."

Apparently, both judge and jury found certain extenuating circumstances brought out in the trial. Presumably, the "bad feeling" between Plaintiff Nichols and Defendant Kraft had existed for some time as a result of various provocations on both men's parts, culminating in the shooting. Probably, the inciting cause is found in the judge's instructions to the jury when he stated:

"The defendant admits he assaulted the prosecuting witness, but undertakes to partially justify it on the ground that the prosecuting witness made some alleged derogatory statement to defendant's wife. So far as that part of the defense is concerned, you are instructed as a matter of law, that if any such alleged statement were made it could not constitute justification . . . (REFUSED Instruction No. 10).

"You are instructed that no mere words, no matter how opprobrious, can constitute provocation sufficient to justify an assault (Instruction 11)."

Chapter 12

New Catastrophes 1918-1919

The new blow, when it fell, came from an unexpected quarter and would have international impact. It started casually enough. People, young and old, had their usual winter colds of sneezing, coughing, and bronchial troubles. Then many suffered aches and pains in their joints and muscles, followed by pneumonia bacilli attacks during the winter and spring of 1918. The disease rapidly infiltrated the ranks of young men in army training camps. Doctors diagnosed this new enemy as the deadly Spanish influenza. Montana's State Health Department began publishing statistics on the incidence and fatal effects of the disease among its citizenry. Ranchers and homesteaders attending to their routine business in Miles City told the papers that rural folk in their area who got sick at all only had a mild attack of the "flu," and the press minimized its ravages in Custer County. But the news columns became increasingly filled with death reports of city and country people.

By September 27, 1918 the Miles City *Independent* was compelled to acknowledge: "Nearly 30,000 Men Now Suffer with Influenza; Rapid Spread of Epidemic Alarms Health Service and Measures Are Being Taken to Prevent Additional

Infection and Carrying of Disease. May Prohibit Public Gatherings All Over Country and Establish a Rigorous Quarantine to Stop Course of Disease which Causes Many Deaths."

Despite joyous news of the Armistice, November 11, bringing an Allied victory and war's end, the health catastrophe now threatened the nation. Indeed, the menace would prove worldwide, resulting in 21 million deaths, including 548,000 American civilians and troops. The terrible influenza scourge sweeping the country cut down those in their prime, as well as the very young and old. All schools, churches, and movie theaters in Miles City closed to prevent the epidemic's spread. Medical authorities advised people to stay away from crowds, not to shake hands, and to wear gauze masks over their noses and mouths whenever they went shopping or marketing.

There were also ominous signs of an incipient drought that could presage disastrous results for eastern Montana's rural dwellers. Cattle shipments to market began in August instead of the fall due to the range drying up earlier than usual and poorer prospects for winter feed. Before the war steers brought $80 a head and during the conflict beef cattle prices jumped to $100 a head. On April 16 to 17, the Montana Stockgrowers' Association held their convention in Great Falls instead of the customary meeting in Milestown. E. W. Nichols' name was drawn for the June 1918 term of District Court. Whether he ever served is unknown. Fort Keogh (modern spelling Keough) began buying remounts in 1918 for U. S. Cavalry service at $135 an animal, a decline in price from the preceding year. In 1915 European army buyers had purchased 900 horses a week at an average price of $140 an animal, the weekly sales amounting to $126,000.

Wartime inflation had raised the price of horses for farming and military uses. During the European-U.S. war years of 1914-1918, weekly auction sales of horses were held in Miles City when usually 1500-2500 head were sold to local ranchers, farmers and the foreign governments. The U.S. government bought cavalry horses in 1917 which sold at $150 for remounts (saddle animals for soldiers); $180 for light artillery; and $225

Chapter 12 — New Catastrophes 145

Regarding this picture, Walter Mann wrote the writer (November 14, 1981): "I rode out with a Charlie Parker, Smokey Nichols, Saul Nichols and DeLoss McBride, and we ran a bunch of range horses into the big Nichols pole corral." Bub Nichols on "Goatafro," his gray roping horse, had roped "Redbird" in right foreground, where DeLoss McBride, wearing white chaps, held rope at Redbird's head, back of ears, before bridling horse. Bub was riding Redbird in 1918 when Redbird fell, causing a critical injury that contributed to Bub's death six years later. Bub and DeLoss broke 4-year-old geldings to sell. Note barren rangeland in the North Sunday Creek area. (Courtesy, Walter E. Mann.)

for heavy artillery use, these being draft horses, according to the *Independent*. Like other ranchers, Smokey would drive his salable stock, geldings and barren mares, to the sales yard in mid-week during June to October.

Walter Mann confirmed in a letter to the writer, October 28, 1981: "Smokey was a horse man. I estimate he had about 300 head of range horses, all branded Rafter T on left shoulder. The horse market was good during the period 1914 and 1918. The first world war was on. The French, English, Spanish [Italian?], and others were there buying horses. They had to be 4 to 9 years old, 15 hands at withers for cavalry and 16 hands for light artillery. I should add they had to be sound. They paid $135 and $165, unheard of prices for range horses up to that time. They had to be ridden into the show ring" [probably as proof of having been well broken].

Guy Crandall, manager of the Miles City Horse Sales, told the *American* (October 30, 1913) that the 12,000 head sold had brought from $5 to $250, with broken, hay-fed animals bringing the larger amounts. The same paper stated that 30,000 horses had been auctioned in Miles City by November 23, 1916, and claimed Milestown was then the nation's biggest and most important horse market.

During the stockgrower's prosperous years, Carrie recalled: "In addition to his own horses, Smoky [sic] ran horses for W. C. Ingram of the Miles City Salesyards and for Ed Love.* One year

---

* Ed Love "became a partner in the Miles City Horse Sales Company and with the outbreak of World War I in 1914, started branding horses for shipment to France. One shipment included 10,000 mules, then unknown in France, provoking the French soldiers to comment about 'those longeared horses' " (**Fanning the Embers**, p. 253). When the horse market collapsed after World War I, Ed Love "bought and sold more than one million acres in ranch properties" (**Ibid.**). He also became active in Ford car dealerships in eastern Montana. Along with other business enterprises which brought him the affluence that made possible a $25,000 donation to "Custer County for a chapel at the Custer County Rest Home." His wife Coris and he "wanted to build a church for our many old friends out at the rest home" (**Ibid.**, p. 254).

Walter E. Mann in backyard of residence at Ogden, Utah, winter of 1979. He was born at Fort Keogh in 1900 and was a horse wrangler for Smokey from 1915 to 1920. (Courtesy, Walter E. Mann.)

Mr. Zecker [sic] brought 800 head of Longhorn steers from Texas. The winter was a bad one [possibly 1916-1917]; they were not acclimated and were dying off fast. Becker [sic] asked Smoky [sic] to take over and save what was left. That was a busy winter, but a successful one. . . . We had many happy times and always wound up the summer with a big 'End of the Roundup Dance' " (*Fanning the Embers*, p. 364).

Walter Mann added more specific details about the Becker cattle: "I was at the north side Nichols ranch from time to time during the period 1915 to 1920. I worked for Smokey as horse wrangler during the summer of 1918. In 1917, Ab [sic] Becker, TZ brand, shipped 1200 head of Mexican steers to Miles City and turned them loose north of the Yellowstone River on government land. We were gathering these steers during the summer of 1918 for shipment to the Chicago stockyards. They

Branding the young stock at the UY-Rafter T corral. Bub had roped the colt and Smokey stood ready to help throw him. (Courtesy Mrs. Margaret Mann Nichols.)

only weighed about 700 pounds, looked like they were all horns and tail, and were as wild as range horses.

"Since Smokey had saddle and work horses, wagon, camp outfit, and me, he contracted to gather and ship those steers. My brother-in-law, Bub Nichols, was wagon boss of Smokey's Rafter T horse ranch (as the UY Ranch was known to Mrs. Mann, although Carrie always referred to it as UY). We had a regular chuckwagon with a four-horse team, a cook, five riders, and about 90 head of saddle horses. No night hawk.

"We went north across south Sunday, Thompson, Big and Little Dry Creeks to Jordan, Montana. Then west and south down Littler Porcupine Creek to the Yellowstone. We shipped about 500 head from the stockyards at Paragon on the C.M.&St.P.R.R. (familiarly known as the "Milwaukee" Railroad) and my job was over."*

Along with the flu menace, the Nichols family confronted economic problems of far graver consequences to them. The setback began with declining sales of horses in 1918. That, in combination with the hay shortage in 1917's severe winter, and beginning omens of a drought that would last for five years and bring economic ruin to the state's agricultural industry with a consequent loss of thousands of its rural population, would also reverse the UY's fortunes. The Denny Smiths were more lucky. They had sold their ranch and invested in city income property, The Hyde Hotel.

In addition, Smokey again became involved in legal trouble. The *Independent* (September 20, 1918) noted that "Earl W. Nichols is the complaining witness" against Mrs. Charles Hayes whom he accused of "dogging" (chasing or worrying) his

---

* *A composite based on a letter to author, October 28, 1981, and article in* **Old Timers News**, *Vol. XIX, No. 2, June, 1981, published by R-4 Forest Service Old Timers' Club, Federal Building, Ogden, Utah 84401. (Mr. Mann's reminiscences were written on Thanksgiving Day, November 27, 1980). A more expanded account appeared in* **True West** *magazine, May, 1982, pp. 13-15.*

While Bub held the foal's head, Josh Stewart restrained movement of hind legs, and DeLoss McBride applied the branding iron. (Courtesy, Mrs. Margaret Mann Nichols.)

Chapter 12 — New Catastrophes

livestock on September 15. Mrs. Hayes' case was set for trial in District Court where she was acquitted of the "stock dogging" charge, which was then a criminal offense. UY cattle, she declared, were ruining her garden, so the jury exonerated her. She had been annoyed repeatedly, she testified, by cattle belonging to Smokey Nichols breaking into her garden patch of seven acres and destroying the produce. She had set her two dogs on the cattle to drive them off her property. During one wrangle, she had threatened to have Smokey arrested, but he "hurried into town" to prefer the dogging complaint against her first — a unique twist in a neighborhood dispute. Similar dogging charges were often aired in the press between ranchers and homesteaders.

The winter of 1918-1919 was very mild, with little snow. Unseasonably warm weather continued after the holidays without a snowfall. Smokey and other ranchers were fearful it portended another dry year for the range. A cold snap in March was a welcome relief that could bring moisture.

Other items appearing in the papers are worthy of note. George E. "Old Man" Petrie, father of Mrs. D. M. Smith, died in April 1919. He was the manager of the Hyde Hotel in Milestown, "a homey place to stop," said their ad. E. W. Nichols was a member of the Montana Horsemen's Organization in April, formed for the purpose of "killing off of the millions of scrub range horses in this state for their conversion into merchantable products in the shape of hides, bone and tallow." Hugh R. Wells of Miles City was president of the association (*Independent*, April 25, 1919).

People were still dying of the flu. Telephones were finally installed on the north and south side of town. Hot, dry winds and little rain raised stockgrowers' fears of a return of drought conditions in May. But wool prices remained high throughout the year. Horse sales fell off during the summer's peak business period, some animals selling for as low as $12 a head. Custer County chalked up a record heat wave in June; cattle were reported dying of thirst in neighboring Rosebud County.

In the midst of discouraging prospects for cattle and horse breeders, another blow fell on the UY boss. County Attorney Frank Hunter signed a District Court Complaint, November 14, 1919, on behalf of John Finlayson and Alec C. McRae, plaintiffs, vs. Earl Nichols and John Doe, "whose true name is unknown," defendants. Finlayson and McRae alleged that "during the past year prior to the filing of this action" they were the lawful owners of 250 head of mixed ewes branded a red horseshoe on their backs and lambs branded a horseshoe in black on their backs, "also some ears slit." Total value of the sheep they claimed was $1800, or $6 per head.

The plaintiffs further charged that all of the animals were "unlawfully detained in the unlawful possession of the said defendants," even though before the action's commencement, the plaintiffs had personally written the defendants, "according to law," demanding the repossession of all their personal property. The defendants had refused to deliver the sheep and still retained possession of them "to the plaintiffs' damage in the sum of Five Hundred dollars ($500.00)" because they were "obliged to expend more than Fifty dollars ($50.00) in the pursuit and recovery of their said property." The plaintiffs demanded judgment either for the return of the sheep "or in lieu thereof" $1800 for the animals' value; damages of $500; plus $50 for expenses incurred, and "costs of the suit."

Also on November 14, Attorney Hunter signed a District Court Requisition order to "A. B. Middleton, Sheriff of Custer County," directing him to take the 250 head of mixed ewes and lambs from the defendants' possession and restore them to the plaintiffs. On November 17, 1919 the action was dismissed as settled.

Since the sheep case is another gap in the interviews with Carrie in 1934, the circumstances are unknown to the author. Nor could Margaret Reid, District Court Deputy Clerk, supply any additional information when questioned in September of 1980. None of the newspapers examined by the writer mentioned the lawsuit, so speculation about specific details of the reasons leading to the court action would be futile. It should be pointed out, though, that Smokey was not charged with grand larceny for theft of the sheep.

However, ex-rancher Bruce Mott added the following comments: "Regarding the John Finlayson and Alec McRae matter and the talk that was going around. In 1919 [1918] the summer was extremely dry and feed was short. On October 8th we experienced a real bad snow storm which caught the Finlayson-McRae sheep on the trail to Miles City to deliver their lambs. During the storm the band became scattered and the bunch that Smokey had drifted on to his place. I don't think Smokey had any thought of keeping the sheep other than to try and collect a little money from the Scotch sheepmen for being Scotch sheepmen"(letter to the author, October 20, 1981).

Chapter 13

The Tragic Drought 1919-1920

Throughout the dry fall of 1919 and the mild winter and spring of 1920, Carrie worried about another dry year and its impoverishing effects on the UY Ranch, especially on Smokey's ability to pay his debts and his desperate struggles to remain solvent.

Half-hopefully, she stood on the kitchen porch one late July morning. A flash of lightning followed by a thunder clap in the west and the tantalizing smell of moisture in the air had brought her out of the hot kitchen. She glanced up at the brassy blue sky, then turned to look northwest where thunderhead clouds were building on the horizon.

"Every day since March," she recalled, "the sun shined, either part or all day long. Not a drop of water, though, had fallen on those rare cloudy days. A dry, scorching wind blew daily over the range fanning my cheeks as from a blastfurnace. Every year till this one *some* seasonal rains had come."

Gazing at the withered brown, rolling hills, she saw the wind catch up dust-devils and spin them crazily over the slopes down into a coulee. Mostly the air was filled with powdery dust. Her throat felt choked with the acrid taste of it. The wind made a hollow, whining sound as it blew through leafless cottonwoods and willows along Sunday Creek.

Suddenly, a miracle took place — a cloud obscured the sun. Carrie glanced in a surge of hope aloft. Then, as usual, her shoulders dropped. She might have guessed it. Just another great swarm of grasshoppers flying through the dust-fogged air. In frustrated rage she shook her fist at them, recalling the garden she had planted and irrigated with water pumped by hand from the well, but the seeds had never sprouted. Grasshoppers had rushed like a tidal wave over everything, devouring every green shoot, stripping leaves from the sagebrush, trees, and greasewood. They even settled on the house, as though they would draw nourishment from the wood.

There were bleached stones in the bed of the creek. No longer did it flow in a constant stream. She could notice a visible shrinkage daily in the few stagnant and shallow pools that remained. In a matter of days the creek would be dried up. As the Indians used to say, the drought-demon stalked the land and wreaked havoc on stock and wild creatures.

At the Stockgrowers' Convention Carrie had observed signs of panic among ranchers over the prolonged hot, dry spell. Miles City had been gaudily decorated with bunting and the colorful parade of cowboys and cowgirls had been held as usual. But the carefree gaiety and hilarity of other years was replaced by an air of doom. Stockmen and their wives halfheartedly tried to be, on the surface, like the old gay crowd of prosperous times. Underneath, Carrie sensed their foreboding and their hysterical grasping for laughter before disaster overcame them.

Already Smokey reported that springs, which never before had failed, had ceased to bubble out of the parched earth. Indeed, even the country's largest rivers were being practically reduced to trickles. Smokey and the boys were riding over the range, feverishly digging out the few remaining mud-choked springs. They sank holes in the creek bed in hopes of finding enough water to save the heifer crop and the best saddle stock. As summer dragged on, most of the older cattle became tottering skeletons, too weak to paw for the life-giving water. Smokey had early sold the feeblest cows, steers, and old bulls, but the price offered by the government had dropped ridiculously low. Nesters and wealthy ranchers fared alike, except that "cattle barons" suffered the heaviest losses.

Each time thunder rumbled sullenly in the distance, though, and banked clouds edged over the horizon rim, Carrie rushed hopefully to the porch. Still the hot wind blew. Going back into the kitchen, she would ask herself, "In the name of a merciful God, how long will this plague last?" At least it took her mind off her other troubles.

The hot, dusty, wearisome days dragged on, the country becoming more denuded and desolate, though that hardly seemed possible. Early fall proved an endless nightmare of dust, wind, grasshoppers, and dying cattle. Emaciated to skin and bones, they staggered near the fences and wasted their feeble strength in a piteous bawling for water. Every time Carrie looked at their black, swollen tongues, their eyes bulging almost out of the sockets and flaming like balls of fire, she retched at the sight. In desperation the dying brutes ate mud in the creek bed. As their wobbly strength gave way they sank, at last, into a merciful death. The sight imprinted on Carrie's mind a picture that would never be banished.

The cowboys could not overtax the horses by dragging away the carcasses, so they lay and putrefied. Soon the stench from their decaying bodies poisoned the air. Carrie might have lost her sanity had she not learned to close a door of her mind to incidents occurring the day before. She looked forward with the thought: "Tomorrow will be another day!" But stress and family troubles turned the last of her black hair pure white, in contrast to her heavy black eyebrows and youthful dark eyes.

At first, most owners skinned the dead animals, then the price of hides went so low it no longer paid them for the effort. She shuddered to think how humans could have gone on living if nature had not provided scavengers. Every time she saw coyotes or gray wolves gorging themselves, she felt humbly grateful.

She even had a friendly feeling for buzzards wheeling in circles overhead before lighting on the carrion. The noisy chatter of magpies became a welcome sound as they lit on the fences before they, too, joined in the macabre feast.

Each time Smokey rode home from an inspection of his stock, he told Carrie it was a cussed shame to see the range littered with carcasses. He wished the war had lasted through "this damn drought" when beef prices were high and wheat went to two dollars a bushel.

The UY's last band of horses Smokey reported in scrawny condition. The best of the herd he fed on scanty portions of chopped straw mixed with hay, and gave even scantier rations of water from the artesian well on the home ranch. Water had become so precious that Carrie no longer used it for scrubbing floors or washing dishes. Instead, she scoured the dishes clean with sand from the creek bottom. Dust blown through the air by constant wind ground into the floor and curtains, and sifted grit into flour and sugar bins. These things she considered minor inconveniences to endure when water represented the difference between life and death. This season, even had there been a yield of buffaloberries and chokecherries, she couldn't have spared the water to make them into jelly and jam. But Smokey found it necessary to butcher a calf, fattened for the purpose, and she canned the meat. Part of it went to the bunkhouse, the rest the family ate.

Finally, Smokey and other ranchers mortgaged their places, some to the limit, so they could buy hay and grain from the government. There were no government subsidies then. After Smokey returned from his last trip into Miles, he told Carrie he hadn't another thing left to mortgage, unless he tossed in the shirt on his back — and his wife. Only the faintest shadow of a grin appeared in his eyes.

For months he had been so worried that his infrequent laughter became a cherished relief to her. His face had grown gaunt and lined, his expression haggard from the long strain. With his drooping black mustache, his loss of flesh gave him a doleful look. How aged at fifty-two he appeared to her twenty-six years. The losses of horse stock that he suffered from the drought had the most harmful effect on him; he became moody. Carrie had been accused by relatives of being an extravagant household manager. That could well be a contributing cause of Smokey's growing business reverses.

Smokey had one odd trait. Carrie could never fully understand his lack of jealousy toward her men friends. He only disapproved of women friends. He was probably afraid they'd put notions in her head.

Late in September came a heavy rain. At sound of the first drops spattering on the parched ground, Carrie ran outside to let the soft, cooling water drench her to the skin. Soon the clouds let loose a downpour. The boys helped her set out every pail, bucket, and pan that could be spared to catch the precious water. After the vessels filled she went about the housework laughing over nothing. She scrubbed floors and washed all the dishes. Then she put clothes, dishcloths, and sheets into the hand-operated washing machine and kept it going until they were nearly threadbare, but smelled of cleanliness. More carefully she laundered the curtains, although the grime discouraged her of ever whitening them again.

Late in the night, although fatigued to the bone, she soaked in a tub of rainwater, and shampooed her hair until her fingers felt raw.

A few light showers fell that fall, but too late to save the stock. Unless the range got a heavy snowpack in winter, Smokey said, the drought would continue and wipe them out. Occasionally, Carrie saddled her mare and rode over the brown prairie. About the roots of dried grama-grass, she noticed a few struggling green shoots pushing up. One day she headed the horse eastward toward the badlands, happy to be free of the long, hot, confining summer days at the ranch and rid of the stench of rotting carcasses. But skulls of cattle and horses and scattered mounds of whitened bones were gruesome evidence of recent tragic months. Gazing over the familiar country, she beheld the once fertile prairie now become a desolation of barbed wire and bare ground, of squalid gates to open and close.

Many nesters' dugouts and shacks were empty and already tumbleweeds had taken over the abandoned farms. Amid leafless branches of dead young fruit trees, a late meadowlark voiced its song. It sounded to Carrie like a mockery, or a lament. These scenes of ruin appalled her even more than while she was enduring similar experiences. Shakespeare, she remembered, said familiarity breeds contempt. One got used to nature's cruelty when it became a daily occurrence. The realization of how widespread were the ravages of the drought struck home. She wondered how long it would be before the range country would recover from its devastation. True, drought conditions had not hit all places at the same time, nor were they equally destructive everywhere. But maybe things were going to get worse before they got better. By 1910 five million acres of Montana grassland had sprouted with the tarpaper shacks of the nesters. Maybe the good Lord intended the land only for grazing.

Stockmen who had taken advantage of high prices and sold most of their herds didn't have credit to buy more cattle. They'd have to mortgage all their holdings and raise two or more good crops before they could get back on their feet. But what if the drought continued — or got worse?

As often as she could get away from the house that autumn, Carrie visited the roundup camp. It was a miserable affair — scrawny cattle and horses and very little young stock. Smokey and the boys were in the saddle daily looking after the surviving animals. With passing weeks, though, Smokey was given to long moody spells. An urgency seemed to be driving him, wearing him down and prematurely aging him.

There were few homesteaders left on the range, Carrie knew. During the exodus many had abandoned their farms in rickety wagons, some in Model T Fords; others had walked out as hoboes. The 1920 U. S. Census population figure of 548,889, compared to the 1930 census of 537,606, showed that Montana,

Chapter 13 — The Tragic Drought

then the nation's third largest state, had lost 11,283 persons. The farms reverted to the government for unpaid taxes.

Stray animals abandoned by their owners began to turn up with "blotched brands," despite a law regarding "estrays," requiring them to be turned over to county officials so the sheriff could hold an auction sale of unclaimed stock. It was evidence of the desperate ways that nesters and ranchers endeavored to recoup some of their losses and hang on in hopes of better times ahead.

Although Carrie had no proof that Smokey might be doing a little rustling, he could have been keeping it concealed from her. His losses from the drought had been great and he finally had been forced to mortgage everything he owned. It was widely believed that all ranchers, big or little, rustled a bit on the side. She recalled an old range adage: "The longest rope catches the maverick." All big outfits branded mavericks, and some paid their riders to switch brands when it wouldn't prove embarrassing, she had heard. It was a standing joke in the cattle country that many a fortune had been made with only a rope and a branding iron.*

---

* Relatives believe Carrie was uninformed about Montana's strict brand laws. "Blotched brands" would be easily detected by stock inspectors and legal troubles would ensue upon sale of the stock.

Chapter 14

The Aftermath of the Drought 1921

In late fall of 1920, Carrie saddled her mare, intending to ride toward the badlands to think over her problems and get away from the miseries, the aura of despair, and family troubles at the ranch. All were becoming more than she could cope with any longer. Unhappy situations that she had been trying to ignore during her married years now demanded a decision.

She urged the horse into a jog along the lane, then turned eastward. In those days she rode in a shirtwaist, ankle-length riding skirt, and cowboy boots. A red bandana was tied about her neck.

The ideals of her stern old father — blind loyalty to one's pledged word, to see through a course already started — had been indelibly stamped on her young mind. These ideals always had inhibited any irreversible decisions heretofore.

A light wind swept over the plain, bringing the pungent odor of sage. Although the sun shone on hills and coulees, a chill made her shiver as she noted again how burned up everything had become, even worse this year than last. Range fires had been bad again, too. Only a few prairie dogs sat up and cheeped at her intrusion as the mare skillfully avoided their holes. Carrie took off her sombrero and let the wind tumble her heavy white hair.

As the jogging pony topped a slope covered with dried up buffalo grass waving and rustling in the breeze, she startled a band of antelope, not over a quarter mile away. Every head jerked erect, ears outspread. The wind was blowing toward her, so she had not been scented. The pronghorns stood looking in curiosity for awhile, then wheeled in a flash of white rumps and bounded away in windlike fleetness. Several spotted fawns nimbly leaped among their mothers. It was the closest Carrie had ever been to these graceful, wild creatures and the sight thrilled her.

Never had the sandstone buttes that formed the badlands ceased to fascinate her.* Here, as in other parts of eastern Montana and the western Dakotas, she had read, the badlands formed a succession of seamed knolls, fantastic turrets, cupolas, and flying buttresses. Their weird shapes were daubed in barbaric colors as though, it occurred to Carrie's fancy, a celestial artist had gone on a titanic spree and slapped his brush across the landscape, leaving olive-gray streaked with brown, lavender striped with black, orange-rust, and chalk pinnacles capped by flaming scarlet. The rains and snows of many years had washed surface soil from the hills, cutting them into jagged gullies.

A geologist from the state university at Missoula who stopped at the ranch one summer had told Carrie the whole area once had been a great lake bed, the bottom covered by clay and loam mud.** The lake had emptied into the Missouri River, and the passing of ages found vegetation growing. More eons of

---

* *This peculiar and picturesque region was called* **mauvaises terres pour traverser** *(literally bad lands for crossing) by early French-Canadian voyageurs.*

** *In 1913 a geological survey of Montana was made, stated the Miles City* **American**.

Chapter 14 — The Aftermath of the Drought

time had changed the vegetation into coal. Bluffs and buttes had been lashed by winter blizzards and washed by summer cloudbursts, until the slopes became gashed and furrowed by gullies and denuded of greenery. Cottonwoods grew in the stream bottoms, like the trees below the rimrock along which she was riding. Grass grew on the tops of hills or plateaus. She had come across many former green pastures in badland valleys.

There were also large areas where only sagebrush and stunted cedars could manage to exist. Most draws or coulees, though, were filled with nutritious grasses that had supplied forage for cattle, horses, and sheep before the drought.

Here Carrie's reminiscences as told to the author in 1934 ended.

It was Carrie's last ride. Tensions that had been building up in her marriage finally reached a climax. Discord, said relatives, had arisen with Smokey's growing children who, by 1920, had reached young adulthood. Bub was 24, Dutch 22, Nora about 19 or 20, and Bessie 17. Carrie, their stepmother, was only 26. Whatever the final incident was — the straw that broke the proverbial camel's back — which motivated Carrie's decision to leave Smokey, she never revealed to the author. In fact, she never mentioned the rift in the interviews, but intimated that Smokey had died during the drought. Relatives stated that Carrie voluntarily separated from her husband in the fall of 1920, and moved to the Denny M. Smith Hyde Hotel in Miles City.

Carrie in *Fanning the Embers* (p. 365), briefly recalled the economic reasons for Smokey's business reverses which also may have helped to influence her decision: "Henry Ford perfected a small tractor that filled the needs in the cotton fields, always before the big market for Western horses. Cavalry as an Army unit was obsolete. On top of that came the winter of 1919-1920. I need not tell of that but, like many others, at its end we were broke, financially and in spirit. Smoky's [sic] heart and life had been horses. He simply could not understand or survive life any other way. He contracted penumonia and died in the spring of 1921."

The brothers relaxing in happier days. Bub holding his perky young daughter, Nora, and Dutch enjoying a smoke. (Courtesy, Mrs. Margaret Mann Nichols.)

Relatives confirmed that Smokey's case was typical of thousands of others in that region of eastern Montana "as every rancher in Rosebud, Custer, and Dawson counties went broke from a severe winter [1916-1917] and continued drouth" (Letter to author, July 24, 1980, from Mrs. Margaret Mann Nichols).

Apparently, his wife's estrangement proved a shocking blow to Smokey, who tried to effect a reconciliation. Carrie remained adamant. Although without funds, she determined to get a job in town.

Meanwhile, financially destitute himself, Smokey's physical condition also deteriorated, doubtless aggravated by stress and worry. In March 1921, he became seriously ill, according to relatives, so his sons Bub and Dutch brought their father to a Miles City doctor who put him in the hospital "with a severe case of penumonia." During his initial convalescence, Smokey stayed at a hotel in town and never returned to the ranch which his sons operated.

His death certificate states that Dr. William H. Buskirk attended him at the Miles City Hospital from April 8 to May 11 when, early in the morning, he died of "acute septic endocarditis," with contributory complications from "pneumonia and emphysema," following an operation on April 20. Funeral services were conducted by undertaker M. H. Wallace, who interred Earl Willard "Smokey" Nichols in the Catholic Cemetery on May 13. An anonymous donor supplied the money for the funeral expenses and the cemetery plot. The tragic combination of circumstances is a realistic commentary on how "broke" one eastern Montana rancher became after livestock prices declined, and the state suffered a severe winter season and a prolonged drought.

Smokey's granddaughter, Norah Nichols Randolph, eulogized her grandfather as "a good-looking, charming man with great appeal for women. His life was a sad one. He was a fine, handsome, loving man who worked desperately hard all of his life and died with his dreams gone, lonely, broke, and brokenhearted" (Letter to author, August 7, 1980).

An obituary notice appeared in the Miles City *American* (May 12, 1921, p. 4): "Earl W. Nichols, known throughout this section as "Smokey" [sic] Nichols, is dead. He was 53 years old and will be missed by all who knew him. His home was on North Sunday Creek 13 miles north of the city and he was a successful stockman. He had been sick since February and his death was due to pneumonia. He leaves a wife and four children, two boys and two girls."

It is unknown to the relatives whether Carrie ever visited Smokey during his last illness, though his sons and Bub's wife did. Smokey's last will and testament, dated May 10, bequeathed to his wife "Carrie J. Nichols, a one-third share of all [his] real property" (total value $2000), but because the "whole spread was mortgaged, even the horses and cattle, Carrie was left without a penny," relatives informed the writer. Carrie told her stepdaughter-in-law that Ed Love, one of the operators of the Horse Sales yard, gave her $500 so she was able to attend business college in town and pay her hotel room rent.

"Some time in the spring or early summer of 1922," she

departed for Southern California, where she stayed "with Smokey's sister, Mrs. Anna Olmstead" until the relationship "ended in a battle royal." Then she lived for a time with Mrs. Rebecca Parker Orr, a former South Sunday Creek neighbor, until "hard feelings" again caused a break in friendship. After that she married Val Lucas, an AEF veteran of War I who died in Los Angeles from gassed lungs in 1935 or 1936.

Smokey's demise ended a memorable segment of Carrie's ranch life in Montana. Like John Boyle O'Reilly, though, she recalled its troubles, tribulations, and bright intervals in later years with smiles, not tears. It was the memory of the pleasant little things that she liked best to dwell upon, like those summer evening interludes of happier days.

When household tasks were finished she often sat on the back porch in the long twilight, resting head and shoulders against the post, awaiting Smokey's and the boys' return to the house after their chores were done and all would join in a game of horseshoes. The Maltese cat lay curled up in her lap, contentedly purring. The black cat sat beside her, licking his paws and washing his face. Shep was down in the meadow on doggy business of his own. As the sky paled to saffron yellow and greenish blue at the horizon, a breeze rose, the air freshened, and sage on the farther hills took on purple shadows. An aromatic blend of country smells — new-mown haystacks, spiced with the pungency of sage and prairie grasses — wafted to her in the cooling air.

Down in the brush along the creek bottom an owl hooted and frogs began croaking as dusk softly closed in. A meadowlark sang a sleepy note, a cow bawled for her calf somewhere in the pasture. Far off, a coyote yapped at the first stars to twinkle in the darkening blue of the sky. In a few hours a full moon would shed pale radiance over the range long after the UY Ranch boss and his family were deep in slumber.

"Those were good times — and bad," she smiled when recounting them. "That's life."

In her final comment about her ranch experience, Carrie

declared: "I have always felt it was a great privilege to have lived in Montana before the passing of 'the Old West' and to have known the wonderful people of that time. Home is where the heart is. I still call Montana my home, a vast open land that breeds men and women of sturdy character, open hearts and open minds" (*Fanning the Embers*, p. 365).

Epilogue

As part of this true-life historical narrative of one family's ranch experience on Miles City's north side, what happened, after Smokey's death, to whom, and when, should also be told. Although his last will and testament left the bulk of his estate to his four children, share and share alike, the real and personal property was so heavily mortgaged that, as already mentioned, there were no funds left to bury him.

The final disposal of the UY Ranch is shrouded in doubt. Some clarification appeared in a letter to the writer from Margaret Reid, Deputy Clerk of District Court, Custer County, Montana, May 9, 1980, which stated in part: "I find record of real property in Earl's (Smokey's) Inventory and Appraisement but find no accounting of what happened to it, and it does not show in the Final Accounting. I checked the Assessor's office and found that that property transferred to a Dunlop in 1923 or 1924, but could find no record of a transfer in the county Clerk and Recorder's office. Dunlop did buy a great deal of property at that time on Sheriff's sale so perhaps that may be what happened to this." So much for the ranch.

Of greater interest, perhaps, are the lives and deaths of family members. Carrie survived Smokey, her first husband, by 58 years. After Val Lucas's death, she recalled: "In 1944 I returned to Miles City and married Al Schlichting whom I had known since I first came to Miles City.... He was Miles City's photographer for 38 years. He also played a saxophone in the Miles City band. After our marriage he decided to retire and move to a warmer climate. We located in Chico, California, in 1947. It is a lovely place at the northern end of the Sacramento Valley. Al died in 1964 and I still live on in our home here."

In 1971, the year Carrie wrote the above for *Fanning the Embers* (p. 365), she also mentioned her sister Elsie "and her husband George Griffith. They lived on a homestead near Westmore, Montana, and are now living in Baker, Montana, where they celebrated their 60th wedding anniversary in February, 1968."

The historical record for Smokey's sons is one of tragic deaths. In the spring of 1918, Earl William "Bub" Nichols "suffered a severe injury while working alone rounding up wild range horses north of Forsyth, Montana. He stayed with his horse [Redbird] after it fell so he would not be set afoot and after his horse got up, he finished the job he was doing and stopped in Forsyth for attention from the doctor. Unfortunately, for lack of prompt medical attention at the time of injury, he never made a complete recovery and died May 27, 1924 (age 28).* He left a fine heritage even though his life was short and tragic. His daughter, Nora, is a successful business woman in San Francisco and wife of Hugh Randolph, an editor on the Oakland *Tribune*. His granddaughter received her Master's Degree in elementary education from San Francisco State College at the age of 22 and has entered the teaching profession in California (*Fanning the Embers*, pp. 309-310).

Bub's wife informed the writer that "Sol's [sic] wife Esther was never at the ranch; she taught school during those tough years. They had two children, a boy Paul and a girl Betty Grace [sic] who was only a baby when her father [Dutch] was killed in

---

* *Bub unknowingly suffered a concussion in 1918 in a horse accident. In another horse fall in 1924 his skull was fractured and he died a few days later.*

Saul Nichols and his wife, Esther Elizabeth Nichols, with infant son, Paul, in buggy, taken in Douglas, Arizona, 1924, where family spent a year, 1923-24. (Courtesy, their daughter, Betty Grayce Nichols Kalfell.)

an accident almost identical to the one in which my husband died" (Letter to writer from Mrs. Margaret Mann Nichols, July 24, 1980).

Saul's widow, Esther McGraw Nichols, "was 79 years of age when she died June 29, 1980 [her daughter Betty Grayce gives the date as July 12, 1980, "one month after my mother's birthday, June 12"], and she was buried in the Catholic Cemetery in Miles City along with her husband Sol,* Smokey, and

---

* *Dutch's name in court records was spelled "Saul," the same as a favorite uncle for whom he was named, the writer was told by Tom Colleran who grew up with Bub and Dutch. In a letter to the writer, February 3, 1981, Mrs. Margaret Nichols wrote that Smokey's "brother SOL NICHOLS (his name was always misspelled in papers but he was baptized SOL) continued to live in Fallon until his death."*

Bub Nichols" (Mrs. Margaret Nichols, letter to author August 4, 1980).

The following account of Mrs. Esther Nichols' death and career as educator is from an unidentified newspaper clipping dated July, 1980, in Miles City. Born June 12, 1901, at Creighton, Nebraska, daughter of Patrick and Elizabeth McGraw, she accompanied her parents to Montana in 1917 when they homesteaded in Garfield County. After graduating at the University of Montana in Missoula, she taught in rural schools in Garfield, Petroleum, and Custer counties before serving in 1930 as teacher and later as principal at Garfield Elementary School in Miles City for 36 years. She retired in 1967, having been principal of Garfield School for 24 years.

"Mrs. Nichols was a member of Delta Kappa Gamma, American Association of University Women, the Miles City Women's Club, Montana Institute of the Arts, and the Sacred Heart Church.

"Her husband, Saul Nichols, died in 1928, killed when he was thrown from a horse on their ranch. Surviving are one son, Paul, of Sunburst; one daughter, Betty Grayce Kalfell of El Toro, Calif.; one brother, Glen McGraw of Sacramento, Calif.; five grandchildren; and two great grandchildren" (Clipping, courtesy Walter E. Mann).

Because Saul's daughter was only eleven months old at the time of her father's death, Betty Grayce told the writer in an interview, June 1, 1981, that she knows "very little about my father's early life," and that her mother's brief marriage to Saul terminated by his untimely death was too painful a memory for her to dwell upon.

However, Betty Grayce added by letter to writer, September 13, 1981, "My parents were married Aug. 2, 1923 and went to [Douglas] Arizona sometime after that — in the fall maybe. When they moved to Arizona my mother's father and her two younger brothers had gone with them. Nora (Smokey's older daughter) was living there at that time. My parents might have stayed in Arizona — they certainly seemed happy in all the pictures taken at that time — but my mother's younger brother was burned to death in a tragic accident. So that brought them back 'home' to Montana." While Dutch's parents "had the ranch near Fallon, he went to the small rural school in 1st grade there."

Perhaps Dutch's death inadvertently resulted from a new law. Don Pyle wrote in *Fanning the Embers* (p. 340), "In 1924 the State of Montana passed a law called 'The Wild Horse Law.' The purpose of this was to get rid of all the strays, unbranded and wild horses. The range was overrun with them." Mr. Pyle became a roundup foreman. Dutch's death certificate states that "Saul F. Nichols" was born August 15, 1898 in Montana; his occupation, "stockman," that he "died May 7, 1928, aged 29 years, 8 months, 22 days." Death was caused by a "basal skull fracture (horse fell with him). Informant: Mrs. Saul F. Nichols, 414 Washington St."

An obituary in an unidentified Miles City newspaper, May 10, 1928, adds details to the legal record:

> RIDER RECEIVES FATAL INJURIES. Horse ridden by Sol Nichol [sic], young northside rancher, falls backward with rider whose skull is fractured when head strikes ground.
>
> Sol Nichol, 29 years old, was fatally injured when he was thrown from a horse at Kinsey and his death took place at the hospital here Monday night, he not having regained consciousness from a fractured skull. Nichol was a son of the late 'Smoky' [sic] Nichol and was well known in this section of the state. He had been out rounding up horses and was trying to get them in a corral when the accident happened.
>
> Nichol was riding a half wild horse. The animal was in an unruly temper and while after the horses the animal reared twice in an attempt to dislodge his rider. Nichol kept him under control for a time and the horse was acting better when without warning it reared again. The horse fell

Epilogue 175

Saul's widow, Esther E. McGraw Nichols, taken just after Saul died, 1928, survived by his four-year-old son, Paul Francis, and eleventh-month-old daughter, Betty Grayce. (Courtesy, daughter, Betty Grayce Nichols Kalfell.)

backward. Nichol was carried down with it and was crushed under the animal, his head striking the ground. Other riders went to his assistance and he was rushed to the hospital but his injuries were such hope was not given for his recovery. He was born in [old] Custer County and had been a rider since early boyhood (Clipping courtesy of Walter E. Mann).

In a telephone interview (March 21, 1982), Betty Grayce added a few more details about her father. During her family's interlude in Douglas, Arizona, Saul (Dutch) was employed at a smelter in that mining town. Upon return to Montana, Saul became foreman for Chappell Bros., an Eastern firm which owned a ranch on Sunday Creek just north of Miles City. Dutch used the Rafter T brand on horses that he captured on the open range.

According to the Brand books, Smokey had also used the same brand on his horses by 1906, in addition to the UY brand between 1888 and 1910 and later. His cattle were registered in the brand books by seven brands: UY, Rafter T (T̂), J (left hip), J (left shoulder), ∀ , I H, and ℌ , a sort of reverse S bar S.

The Chappell Bros. (brand CBC), of Rockford, Illinois, began their Montana ranching operations in 1927 at Oswego, where 2500 horses were first branded. According to *Fanning the Embers* (p. 432), "Headquarters were on Sunday Creek, eight miles northeast of Miles City at the old Becker ranch. A roundup wagon left the ranch about June 1 each year and carried on until all colts and horses were branded." About 5000 colts were annually branded on the range. By 1934, 20,000 horses "came off this range which extended from the Missouri to the Yellowstone and from the Red Water on the east to the Musselshell River."

Former Moon Creek rancher Bruce T. Mott substantiated the above in a letter to the writer (May 15, 1982) and added that Chappell Bros. "were in the dog food business and came into this area to purchase horses. They had a packing plant in Miles City where they processed quite a number of range horses during a period of about 10 years. As part of their operations they acquired a ranch located on *main* [North] Sunday Creek known as the old Hugh Wells place. This place had been owned by Abe Becker, a cattle dealer from Sioux City, 1916 to 1921. Becker went broke and the Sunday Creek place was leased to other people until taken over by Chappell Bros. about 1925 or thereabouts. The north side of the Yellowstone at that time was considered open range. This condition continued to June 30, 1932 when the Taylor Grazing District law was passed by

Congress, which ended the Chappell Bros. operation in Montana."

Relatives did not remember the date or place of Smokey's younger daughter Bessie's death in Southern California. Smokey's seven brothers and sisters have also died, except for Smokey's youngest brother William of Woodburn, Oregon, who was age 97 in 1982 (Letter to author from Mrs. Margaret Nichols, August 31, 1982).

As for Anna Egan Nichols, Smokey's first wife, Mrs. Margaret Nichols wrote the writer that she (Anna) "died years ago, possibly in Texas — the last time I saw her was in 1924, a short time after Bub's death. She came into Miles City from Texas. She heard the sad news as she drove up Tongue River. We went out to the cemetery to visit Bub's grave. I gave her Bub's saddle as I knew she could use it and it would give her something important to keep" (August 4, 1980).

Smokey's older daughter Nora and her sister-in-law Margaret became lifelong friends whose working lives ended with retirement. Nora had married Ralph Kuhn who "was killed in Italy, shortly after the troops from North Africa invaded Italy," Margaret Nichols recalled. "Nora was very talented and a very bright person, anything she decided to learn or accomplish she carried through. When I lived in Las Cruces, New Mexico, she lived in Douglas, Arizona, and we got together often. She came over to Las Cruces and took a Civil Service Examination (which I was authorized to give for the government). She got a job in the U. S. Forest Service in Colorado, then I went back to Montana as my father and mother were still living in Miles City and my father was very ill. I took a government job in Helena, Montana, and the Forest Service transferred Nora to a job in Missoula, Montana. She was familiarly known in the Forest Service as "Jimmie" Kuhn. We had many happy times together and lots of wonderful trips, both by car and plane. Nora had her own plane and a pilot's license. [After her retirement] Nora died in 1976. She was cremated and her ashes sprinkled over the beautiful Mission Range south of Flathead Lake" (Excerpted from letters

Snapshot taken in 1934 near Missoula, Montana, of left to right, Mrs. Esther Nichols, Betty Grayce, 7, Paul, 10, holding his aunt's Scottie dog, and the children's Aunt Nora Nichols Kuhn, sister-in-law of their mother. (Courtesy, Betty Grayce Nichols Kalfell.)

to author by Mrs. Margaret Nichols, August 4, and August 24, 1980).

Before she was widowed by Bub's early death, Margaret "went to work as a civil service employee in 1920 to help our finances" when livestock prices sharply declined (Letter to author, July 24, 1980).

After Bub died in May, she and her six-year-old daughter Honora left Miles City in July 1924.

> I worked for the government in Mancos, Colo. and Roswell and Las Cruces, N. M. I returned to Montana in November, 1929, because of the illness of my father, Michael Mann. The depression was just beginning and few

jobs were available. I was able to get a government position in Helena, Mont. and worked there until 1947, making many trips to Miles City to visit my mother, Rosa, Mann, and old friends. In 1947 I transferred to San Francisco where Honora and her husband, Capt. Hugh Randolph, had settled after his discharge from the Army. I am retired now and usually spend part of each year in Montana because it is always home to me" (*Fanning the Embers*, 1971, p. 310).

Meanwhile, Mrs. Ernest Schwabenthal, Carrie's neighbor in Chico, California, looked after Carrie's affairs when she had a stroke. Carrie had been living alone after her third husband Al Schlichting's death in 1964. She sold her home and spent her last days in a convalescent hospital in Chico, where she died August 27, 1979. In a telephone interview, August 1980, Mrs. Schwabenthal told the writer that she had acted as executrix of Carrie's estate. She added that during Carrie's last illness, Elsie preceded her sister in death by about three months, also as a result of a stroke.

As in the case of the Nichols family, the American dream of many rural people in eastern Montana became an American tragedy through the juxtaposition of a depressed economy and concomitant adverse weather conditions. Most of those people have departed on the sunset trail across the Great Divide, but they are remembered in the hearts of their relatives and friends. One survivor, a retired schoolteacher, expressed the legacy to posterity of these rugged modern pioneers in the poem "Retrospection":

> Oh, pioneers of yesteryears,
>   Your hopes, your joys,
>   Your hidden fears.
> Little cabins tumbled down,
> Roofs caved in and chimneys gone.
>   Wagon tracks, faint outlines now,

Weeds hide hayrake and a plow.
Good times, bad times echoing through
Years gone by but not forgotten,
Bitter, sweet but treasured true.
    A blessed heritage you have given;
    Our heartfelt thanks we offer you.

Gladys (Barstow) Laurie, *Fanning the Embers*, p. 574. (Courtesy, Range Rider Reps, Miles City, Montana.)

Genealogical Chart 181

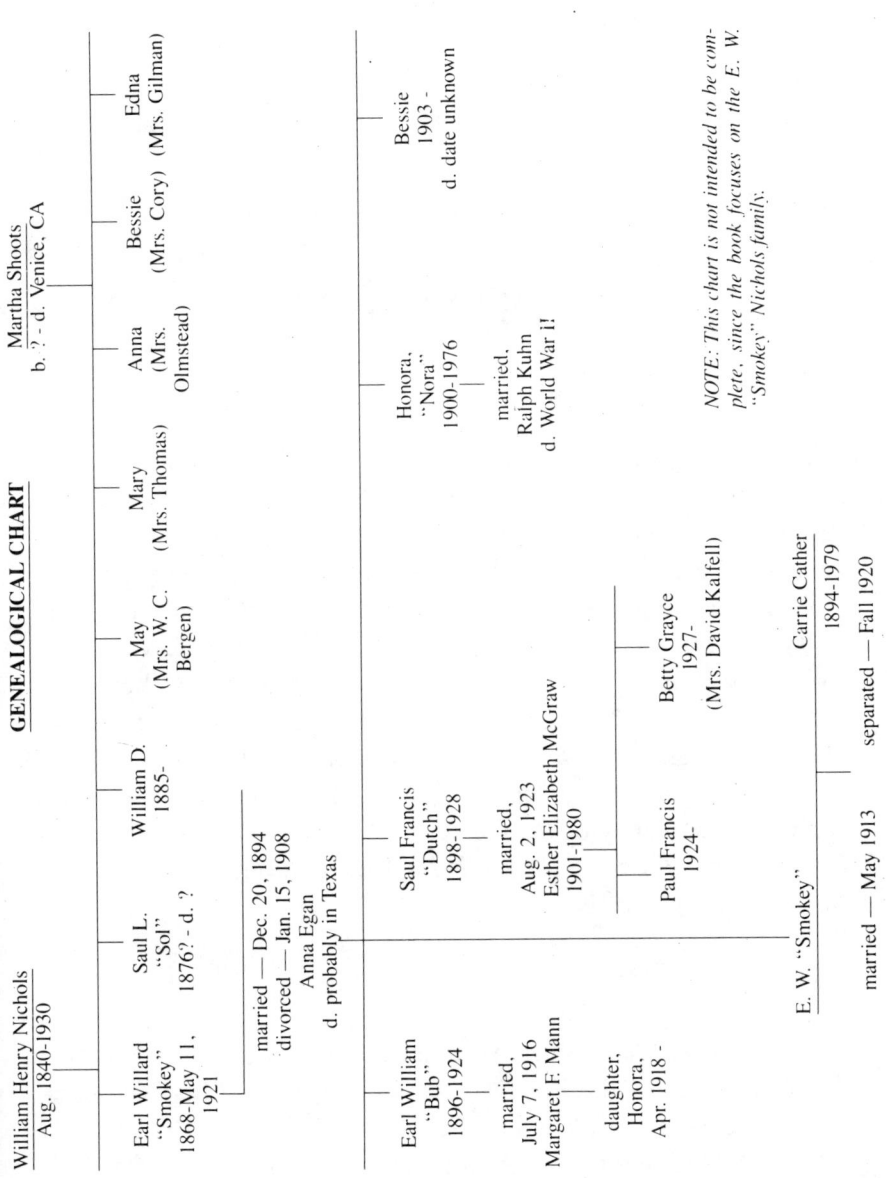

Appendices

Mrs. Margaret Mann Nichols, Bub's widow, supplied many personal reminiscences of the UY Ranch story, first as a girl growing up at Fort Keogh, and later living on the ranch as Bub's wife until the drought and the UY's business reverses caused her "during those tough times" to seek a government job in Miles City. Memories of people and events of those bygone years are told here mostly in chronological sequence because they give revealing sidelights on homesteading and ranching on North Sunday Creek. She was also a member of the Range Rider Reps, whose purpose was to preserve through rural settlers' written records the history of the Custer County region in the community history, *Fanning the Embers*. Her memoirs are somewhat abridged.

* * *

Smokey's father, William Henry Nichols, was a Confederate Army veteran of the War of Secession. He spent his last years with one of his oldest children, May Nichols (Mrs. W. C. Bergen), and died in Honolulu in 1930, aged 90. May had married a merchant seaman from New England who had fallen in love with the Islands and with May, who had gone there to teach school. May has grandchildren still living there. Her one son came to the mainland and became a doctor. He married in Honolulu and had three girls and one boy. His son became a veterinarian and is employed on the Island of Hawaii's Parker ranch, one of the largest cattle ranches in the world, where he heads the many veterinarians on the ranch's staff.

* * *

Bub told me that when he was a very young boy, about 10 or 11, and was living alone with his father at the sandstone slab ranch house on Dry Creek, Smokey and some other men were gathering wild horses to corral. One horse kicked Smokey in the jaw, breaking it, and knocking him unconscious. The men hitched up a team to a farm wagon, put in a bed roll, placed Smokey on it, and took him at least forty miles to Miles City for a doctor. Bub was alone at the ranch a long time before he heard if his father lived. Smokey had quite a bad scar on his cheek.

* * *

Robert "Tuffy" Arneberg was at the ranch part of the time with Bub and Sol. Robert was still in his teens and very bright, but was able to spend little time in school. I have in my files a picture of him which he had sent to Bub. He is wearing his first white Navy uniform, and has an expression on his face, that says "I'm so lonesome to be back in Montana." He lived alone after retirement in Coarse Gold, California. His dad came there and stayed with Robert for a time, but I think he finished his days in a Masonic home.

* * *

I knew Mina (Minnie) Arneberg, the oldest girl, who stayed with me a short time in April or May of 1918 when I returned to the ranch with my small baby Nora. If there were 14 Arneberg children, I only knew Robert, Carl, and Mina. What became of the other eleven, I have no idea. [Carrie mentioned only the seven Arnebergs as narrated in Chapter IV. Possibly, the others had died in infancy.]

* * *

After Carrie left the Smiths' in great anger, she moved in at the Dixon ranch, not far from the Smiths, on Sunday Creek near the 12-Mile Bridge on the only road that went all the way to Jordan. As far as I know, she stayed at Dixons' until school was out, then returned to Wisconsin where Smokey went to marry her.

* * *

About young Sol's name. Smokey's brother was *Sol* L. Nichols, because his mother romantically referred to the *sun* when he was baptized. Then when Smokey's baby son was to be baptized, the priest was told that the infant's first name was Sol, like his uncle's, but the priest had never heard of such a thing. So he spelled the name *Saul*, after the biblical apostle, on the baptismal record. When Betty Grayce's brother came along the mistake was continued and he was called Saul. He never liked the name and later changed it to Paul. My own daughter was baptized Honora Nichols, from which the nickname Nora comes. Of course, she was named after her Aunt Nora (Honora).

* * *

One day while Bub and his dad were trying to lift a wagon box, Bub slipped on the ice and broke his leg close to the hip. Dr. Buskirk took care of him in the hospital. I often went to see him and took fudge I had made. But we were both so shy and sort of embarrassed that we couldn't think of anything to say.

* * *

Smokey was a man's man but always respectful to women. He did have a great deal of attention from them and could have had most of them that he met. He was always kind to me and I liked him very much. I doubt if Carrie ever found another man equal to him. She told me about all the men she met who wanted to marry her. Carrie often spoke of Smokey (after I looked her up in Chico) and spoke of him as *Old Smokey*, and said the only man she ever loved was Lucas, her second husband. [Had time erased the image of Bill Griffith from her memory, one wonders?]

* * *

In 1918 some of the outfits that had lots of horses and few cattle (like Smokey) tried an experiment of butchering and eating horse meat. A yearling colt's hindquarter was said to be tender and good but had a sweet taste, different from beef. I don't recall if the experiment was repeated. [Horse meat was, and still is, popular in Europe.]

* * *

Bub was injured bringing in a bunch of wild horses to corral in 1918. When his horse fell, Bub stayed with it, as the animal was not gentle and he might not have been able to catch it. Also, Bub may have been unconscious for a short time before the horse got up. He finished corralling the wild horses and as his knee was hurt, he stopped in Forsyth where the doctor bandaged his knee. Unfortunately, he didn't tell the doctor that his sight was blurred or that he had trouble hearing the doctor's voice. About a month later he began to suffer blackouts for short periods. A long time later, Dr. Andrus told me that what Bub had was a *concussion* and if he had been put in the hospital and treated at the time of the accident he would have been all right.

* * *

Carrie went to Wisconsin to visit her folks the winter of 1918. She wrote Smokey that she would come back when he got rid of me and the baby. Smokey told me about the letter, so when she came back I was evicted — you might call it that. Bub came to town with me but he could not find any work he could do on account of the blackouts he suffered.

* * *

As for Mrs. Denny Smith, I haven't the foggiest idea what her first name was. They lived on Sunday Creek south of Smokey's place. Denny and Smokey as neighbors worked out their problems. I had very little contact with Mrs. Smith but saw more of Denny. That man Becker who came out to Montana with the idea of getting rich in ranches and cattle bought the Denny Smith place for $25,000. That is where Smokey looked after the cattle Becker shipped up from Texas and which were not used to cold weather.

The Smiths bought a large, expensive car which Mrs. Smith burned the motor out of when she got stuck in a creek. With what they had left they made a payment on the Hyde Hotel to Dr. Hyde's wife. That's where Carrie stayed after she left the ranch and seemed to be very friendly with Mrs. Smith, in spite of her falling out with her before. Carrie was there when Smokey died. I don't think she had a paying job in Miles City. She did start to go to the one and only business college that I attended, but I was already working. I had passed the Civil Service examination and was employed, first at the Miles City Post Office, later by the Interior Dept., U.S. Land Office, where those Eastern people came in and filed on homesteads and ruined the country for large ranches.

Carrie may have worked at the Hyde Hotel to earn room rent. I never heard a word about her or from her, as the boys were out on the range gathering some of the horses already mortgaged (like all ranchers), and the lovely horses were shipped for dog food. After she married Lucas her parents died and she inherited a bit of money from the sale of the farm. She told me they lost the money in a bad investment. After Lucas died there was plenty of work in connection with war materiel in California. I would have gone to see Carrie when I went to California to visit my sister and also Smokey's sister, Ann Olmstead. Ann told me that Carrie was living nearby but didn't indicate that she would care to take me to visit her, so I never knew any more about her until I made a trip to Chico. She seemed not a particularly happy person (Schlichting had already passed away and left her enough money to live on).

* * *

While Smokey lay dying in the Miles City hospital, surrounded by his brother Sol L. Nichols from Fallon, Bub, and Dutch, his daughter Nora was en route from Arizona but did not arrive until after the funeral. Bub told me that the last words Smokey said were: "Nora will soon be here. I can see the dust on the road from the wagon." His mind went back to the old days when you always knew if you were going to have company as you could see the dust from the dirt roads. Nora was working for the government in the Southwest.

* * *

Bub was injured in another fall from his horse on the Lockie ranch about the latter part of May 1924. The Lockies brought him to town and I took him to the hospital. His skull was fractured and he never regained consciousness, only lived a few days. I was there with him until about 11 o'clock and he died the following morning about daybreak. I loved Bub and had no desire to marry anyone else. The best way to prove it was by bringing up his daughter in the way he would have wanted. Nora and I had a wonderful life and I never was unhappy but cheerful and interested in everybody and everything that came along. Bub's sister Nora and I always had a close relationship and I was there in Missoula with her when she died in 1976. In July 1924, I accepted a government job in Mancos, Colorado.

* * *

Shortly after Bub's funeral his mother Anna came to the house. She had just ridden in a truck all the way from Texas with her second husband, McGrath. As they came down Tongue River someone told her of Bub's death. I took her out to the cemetery to his new grave beside Smokey's and she put her head down and cried. I felt so sorry for her. I cried and held her in my arms. She was tired from the long hard trip and shocked by the sad news. Later on I asked her if she would like to have Bub's saddle. I knew that was something she could cherish. I never saw her again but I was fond of her.

Index

Compiled by Terry G. Colbert

— A —

American Association of University Women, 173
Andrus, Dr. W. W., 139, 185
Arneberg, Carl, 49, 81, 184
Arneberg, Earl, 44
Arneberg, Eric, 49, 81
Arneberg, Maria, 43-44, 46, 48-50, 55, 63, 81
Arneberg, Minnie, 43-44, 46, 48-50, 55, 63, 81
  first name given as Mina, 183-184
Arneberg, Oscar, 48-49
Arneberg, Robert (real name of Tuffy Arneberg), 183-184
  adopted by Ray Lowe, 49
Arneberg, Tuffy, 48
  adopted by Ray Lowe, 86
  See also Arneberg, Robert

— B —

Babe (nickname for Mrs. Denny M. Smith), 42, 51
  See also Smith, Mrs. Denny M. "Sadie"
Badlands, 164
Baker, Montana, 91, 171
Becker, A.
  buys Denny M. Smith ranch, 140
  Ab Becker, 147
  Abe Becker, 176
Abe Becker, purchase of Denny M. Smith ranch, 186
Biddle School, xii
Big Dry Creek, xiii, 71
Birth of a Nation, The, 136
Bitter Root River, xii
Bitter Root Valley, xii
Brands
  CK, 38
  Flying Y, 85
  Hat X, 38
  Rafter T, 146, 176
  XIT (Ten-in-Texas), 38
  TZ, 147
Box and Arrow Ranch
  called the Bow Gun, 38
Boyd, Dr., 83, 85
Bub
  See Nichols, Earl William "Bub"
Bull Creek, 136
Bull Moose ticket, 22
Buskirk, Dr. William H., 184
  and Smokey's death, 166

— C —

Cather, Carrie, 1, 2, 10, 16, 32, 55, 72, 81, 87, 133, 146, 185
  after leaving Smokey, 186-187
  ambivalence toward Smokey, 100
  and Bub's elopement, 127-129

and drought of 1919-1920, 155-161
and Smokey's attentions, 57
and winter of 1916-1917, 136
arrival in Montana, xiii, 1-11
at High-Pockets' Ranch, 29-35
attends dances with Smokey, 56
attraction to Bill, 10-11, 14-16
begins teaching, 37-52
Bill's proposal, 22-24
Christmas at the Smiths, 57-59
compassion, 93-104
complains to school board about Sadie, 51
contrasted with Sis, 9-10
domestic disputes, 104, 111
eviction of Margaret Mann Nichols, 186
father, xiii, 1-2, 29, 32
feelings for region, 2, 7-8, 27
first day as teacher, 45-49
gaps in reminiscences, 86, 129, 152
hopes of hearing from Bill, 80
interviews with, xii
isolation at UY Ranch, 90
learns of Sis's deception, 117-120
leaves Smokey, 163-169
marriage to Al Schlichting, 171
marriage to Smokey, 79-80
marriage to Val Lucas, 168
meets "Dutch" Nichols, 107-110
meets Smokey, 53
memories of Bill, 115
memories of Smokey, 67
move from Smith to Dixon ranch, 184
mother, 2, 32
murder of Slav woman, 95-101
New Year's Eve dance at the Campbells', 59-62
nicknamed "Touch-me-not," 28-29
parting from Bill, 34-35
plans to write Bill about dances with Smokey, 56
reaction to vulgarity, 8
related to Willa Cather, 9
ride to the Smith place, 39-42
showdown with Sadie, 63-65
showdown with Sis, 124-126
sleeping arrangements at the Smith place, 44-45

summary of life, xiii-xiv
teacher's examinations, 29-30, 32-33
turns from Bill to Smokey, 58
visit to Sis in 1916, 115-126
white hair, 99,117
writes to Bill about Sadie, 51
See also Griffith, Bill
         Griffith, Elsie Cather
         Lucas, Carrie Cather
         Nichols, Carrie Cather
         Nichols, Earl Willard "Smokey"
Cather, Elsie "Sis"
  See Griffith, Elsie Cather "Sis"
  See also Cather, Carrie
Cahter, Willa
  related to Carrie Cather, 9
Cavvy, 18-19
Cedar Creek, 75
Chappell Brothers, 176
Chicago Stockyards, 147
Chico, California, 171
Clansman, The, 136
Clark, Bill, 75
Clinton, Montana, 90
C.M.&St.P.R.R. (the "Milwaukee" railroad), 149
Coarse Gold, California, 183
Cole, Pat (great-grandson of Sol L. Nichols), 90
Colleran, Tom, 67-68
Crandall, Guy, 146
Creighton, Nebraska, 173
Crow Rock, 136
Custer County, 39, 130, 133, 173, 175, 182
  and the flu of 1918, 143
  heat wave, 151
Custer County Board of Education, 33
Custer County High School, 127

— D —

Dakota Territory, 38
Daly, Charles, 138
Dawson County, 39, 72
DeCarle, John E., 141
Deer Lodge penitentiary, 138
Delta Kappa Gamma, 173
Dipping, 20

Index

Dixon, Evaline (Mrs. Dixon), 63, 90
   related to Elizabeth Huff Mott, 65
Dixon, Norma, 49, 63, 81
Dixon, Walter, 65, 81
Documentation, x-xii, xiv
Dorothy Taylor, xii
Double Diamond D-Bar Dot Ranch, 20
Douglas, Arizona, 173, 176-177
Drexels (neighbors to Dorothy Taylor), xii
Dry House Creek, 71
   Smokey's former ranch, 83
Dutch
   See Nichols, Saul F. "Dutch"

— E —

El Toro, California, xiv, 173
Errick, L. (or I.), 77
Errick, William, 77

— F —

Farr, George W., 69
Fallon, Montana, 69, 174, 187
   birthplace of Bub Nichols, 71
Finlayson, John, 152
Flathead Lake, 177
Ford, Henry, 165
Ford, Model T, xiii
   advent of, 82
Forest Service, U.S., 177
Forsyth, Montana, 171, 185
Fort Keogh, 37, 87, 182
   birthplace of Margaret Mann Nichols, 127
   birthplace of Walter E. Mann, 110
   buys horses from Smokey, 56, 117, 144
   modern spelling Keough, 144
Fort Peck dam, 71
Fudge, Bob, xii
   foreman of Hat Ranch, 38

— G —

Garfield County, 173
Garfield Elementary School, 173
Gibb, John, 130
Gill, Arthur, xii
Gilmore, Hi, 85
Gilmore, Ralph, 85
Glendive, 127

Goodall, John W., 75
Great Falls, Montana, 144
Great War, The
   and horse market, 146
   war effort, 139
   wartime inflation, 138, 144
Griffith, Bill, 6, 7, 9, 15-16, 22, 79, 185
   after Carrie's marriage, 115, 123
   and Carrie's arrival in Montana, 3-4
   as singer, 7, 14-15, 17, 24, 58
   at the Vandervoots', 5, 7
   courtship of Carrie, 13
   delivers results of teacher's examination, 33
   failure to write, 57
   in charge of Griffith homestead, 28
   jealously, 29, 31
   proposal to Carrie, 22-24
   visits Carrie at Titus ranch, 30
   See also Cather, Carrie
          Griffith, Elsie Cather
          Spring round up
Griffith, Elsie Cather "Sis," xiii, 2, 82, 111, 127, 171
   and Carrie's arrival in Montana, 3-5
   appearance in 1916, 117
   attraction to Bill, 7, 14
   death, 179
   deception, 120
   hiring out to Titus, 27
   homestead described, 9
   irritability, 15
   jealously, 3, 10-11, 14, 16-17, 24-25, 31, 34
   letters from, 56, 58
   marriage to George, 11
   pregnancy, 10, 13, 17, 32, 57
   two children, 117
   urges Carrie to visit, 115
   See also Cather, Carrie
          Griffith, Bill
          Griffith, George
          Spring round up
Griffith, George (Elsie Cather's husband), 2-3, 7, 14, 33, 115, 171, 124
   building of homestead, 9
   marriage to Sis, 11
   signs of age, 116
Griffith homestead, 82

Grimes Creek, 77

— H —
Hall, Harry, 136
Handley, Robert, 90
Handley, Mrs. [Robert], 90
Hat X Ranch, xii-xiii, 38
Hawley, Blanche, 136
Hayes, Mrs. Charles, 149-151
Helena, Montana, 177, 179
Herrick (attorney), 130, 132
"High-Pockets" Titus, 29, 32-33, 82
   why so called, 28
Homestead Act (Bill or Law), 78, 94, 135
Homesteaders, 93-94
   conflict with cattlemen, 38, 94-95, 111-114
   living conditions, 16
   migrant, xiii
   problems of, x, xii
Honolulu, Hawaii, 182
"Honyockers" (Central European immigrants), 38, 95
Horse breeders, 87
Horse meat, 185
Horse sales, 151
Horses, mentioned by name
   Brownie, 54
   Chief, Bill Griffith's horse, 22, 24
   Chris and Seal, 17
   Dewey, saves Dan Lockie's life, 136-137
   Redbird, 171
   Sky Rocket, 114
Howard, Helen Addison
   publications, ix-x
   background, xiii
"Hunky" (Central European immigrant), 95, 101
Hunter, Frank, 130, 152
Hurley, Judge C. C., 141-142
Hyde Hotel, 151, 165, 186

— I —
Ike (Slovakian immigrant), 101-103
Immigration, 91
Influenza, Spanish
   the flu of 1918, 143-144, 149
Ingram, W. C., 146

Ismay, Montana, 28, 33

— J —
Jones, Tom, 133
Jordan, Montana, 81-82, 149, 184
Judith Basin, 38
Junior (child of George and Elsie Cather Griffith), 117, 123

— K —
Kalfell, Betty Grayce (Mrs. David), xiv, 173
   See also Nichols, Betty Grayce
Kirksville, Missouri, 138
Kohrs, Con, 38
Kreuger Creek, 130, 132
Kraft, J. W. (or J. E., or P. W.), 139-142
Kraft, Odessa (Mrs. J. W.), 141
Kuhn, Ralph, 177
Kuhn, "Jimmie," 177
   See also Nichols, Nora (Smokey's older daughter)

— L —
Las Cruces, New Mexico, 177-178
Laurie, Gladys Barstow, 180
Line-camps, 111, 114
Little Dry Creek, 38, 74, 149
   Smokey's original ranch, 71
Little Porcupine Creek, 85, 149
Little Powder River, xii
Little Tongue River, xii
Lockey, Bill
   See Lockie, Bill
Lockie, Bill, 85
Lockie Bors, 85
Lockie, Dan, 85
   marriage to Blanch Hawley, 136
Lockie, Dave, 85
Lockie, George, 85
Lockie, James, Jr., 85
Lockie, John, 85
Lockie Ranch, 187
Logan, Jack, 138
Loney, Pat, 114, 129
Loud, Charles H., 75
Love, Ed., 146, 167
Lowe, Ray
   death of, 86, 141
   guest at Hyde Hotel, 140-141

Index

shot, 82-83, 85-86
Lowe, Tuffy
    See Arneberg, Robert
Lucas, Carrie Cather
    interviews with, ix
    See also Cather, Carrie
Lucas, Val, ix, 185
    death of, 170, 187
    marriage to Carrie Cather, 168

— M —

Mancos, Colorado, 178, 188
Mann, Michael F. (father of Walter E. and Margaret), 110, 178
Mann, Rosa B. (mother of Walter E. and Margaret), 110, 179
Mann, Walter Edward (brother of Margaret Mann Nichols), xv, 86, 110, 140, 146-147, 173, 175
McGrath, Anna Egan Nichols, 188
McGraw, Elizabeth (mother of Esther Nichols), 173
McGraw, Patrick (father of Esther Nichols), 173
McIntire, Dr., 85
McKay, Dan C., 75
McKinzie, John, 130
McLean, John, 129-135
McRae, Alec C., 152
Methods, historiographic, xii
Middleton, A. B., 152
Miles (Miles City), 34
Miles City, Montana, ix-x, 11, 49, 70, 82-83, 85, 110, 114, 127, 130, 133, 136, 138, 146, 153, 156, 166, 170-173, 176-180, 182-183, 186
    and the flue of 1918, 143-144
    birthplace of Bruce Mott, 65
    first roundup, 1914, 88
    horse auctions, 144
    location of Hyde Hotel, 140
    location of Range Riders Museum, 68
    October cattle drive, 86
    sheepraising, 135
Miles City Hospital, 166, 187
Miles City Salesyards, 146
Miles City Women's Club, 173
Milestown (former name of Miles City), 38, 144, 147, 151

Mission Range, 177
Missoula, Montana, ix, 177, 188
Missoula Tourist Camp, xiii
Missouri River, 164, 176
Montana
    settlement of, x
Montana Institute of the Arts, 173
Montana State Health Department, 143
Montana Stockgrowers' Association, 78, 144
Montana, University of (Missoula), 173
Monty, the cook, 16-17, 19-20
Moon Creek, 65
Moon Creek Ranch, 176
Mott, Bruce (grandson of Elizabeth Huff Mott), 65, 114, 135, 153, 176
Mott, C. H. (Larry)
    father of Bruce Mott, 65
Mott, Elizabeth Huff
    related to Evaline Dixon, 65
Mott, Helen J. Henry
    mother of Bruce Mott, 65
Musselshell River, 38, 91, 176

— N —

National Detective Agency, 78
"Nesters"
    and drought of 1919-1920, 157, 160
    and killing of Smokey's horse, 104-105
    plight of, 93-105
    slang for homesteaders, 78, 94
Nex Perce Fork, xii
Nichol, Smoky, 174
    See also Nichols, Earl Willard "Smokey"
Nichols, Anna Egan (Smokey's first wife), 69, 71, 74
    death, 177
    divorce, 77
    receives Bub's saddle, 188
Nichols, Bessie (Smokey's younger daughter), 72, 74, 110, 165
    death, 177
Nichols, Betty Grayce (daughter of Saul F. "Dutch" Nichols), xiv, 111, 171-172, 175, 184

Nichols, Bub
  See Nichols, Earl William "Bub" (Smokey's older son)
Nichols, Bud
  "Bud" error for "Bub", 67
  See also Nichols, Earl William "Bub" (Smokey's older son)
Nichols, Carrie Cather (Mrs. E. W.), xiv
  quest at Hyde Hotel, 140-141
  See also Cather, Carrie
Nichols, Dutch
  See Nichols, Saul F. "Dutch" (Smokey's younger son)
Nichols, Earl
  identity, 69
  See also Nichols, Earl Willard "Smokey"
Nichols, Earl Wilbur
  death certificate, 67
  See also Nichols, Earl Willard "Smokey"
Nichols, Earl Willard "Smokey", 55, 86, 115, 183, 186
  and Bub's elopement, 128
  and Carrie's showdown with Sadie, 64-65
  and drought of 1919-1920, 155, 158-159, 161
  and Ray Lowe shooting, 82-83, 85-86
  as early rancher, 94
  attitude toward nesters, 95, 100, 103-104
  background, 67
  correct name, 68
  death, 165, 188
  documentation, x
  early life, 70-72
  guest at Hyde Hotel, 140-141
  in an era of change, 77-78
  invites Carrie to a dance, 56
  last will and testament, 67, 167, 170
  legal troubles, 74, 129-135, 149-153
  marriage to Anna, 72-74
  marriage to Carrie, 79-80
  offers Carrie use of horse, 54
  outrider shot by nester, 111-114
  personality, 185
  provides Carrie with bodyguard, 81
  registered brands, 176
  sale of horses, 177, 144, 146
  shot by J. W. (or J. E., or P. W.) Kraft, 139-142
  suspected of rustling, 161
  transfers UY brand, 69
  write of *habeas corpus* for Nora, 74
  See also Cather, Carrie
Nichols, Earl William "Bub" (Smokey's older son), 67, 71-72, 74, 149, 165-166, 183
  character, 88
  death, 171-187
  elopement, 127
  injured, 184-185
  moves to town with Margaret Mann Nichols, 186
  Ray Lowe shooting, 83
  routine ranch work, 86
  Smokey's death, 187
  See also Nichols, Margaret Mann
Nichols, Esther McGraw (wife of Saul F. "Dutch" Nichols), 111, 171, 174
  death, 172
Nichols, George, 136
Nichols, Margaret Mann (sister of Walter E. Mann; wife of Earl William "Bub" Nichols, xv, 39, 67, 71, 74, 87, 90, 149, 166, 172-173, 177-178, 182
  arrival of Saul F. "Dutch" Nichols at UY Ranch, 110
  elopement, 127
  eviction, 186
Nichols, May (Mrs. W. C. Bergen), 182
Nichols, Honora (Nora, Bub's daughter), 68, 82, 128, 178, 183-184, 187
  married to Hugh Randolph, 171, 179
Nichols, Nora (Honora, Smokey's older daughter), 72, 74, 110, 165, 173, 177, 184
  death, 187-188
Nichols, Paul (son of Saul F. "Dutch" Nichols), xiv, 171, 173
  christened Saul, 184
Nichols, Saul F. "Dutch" (Smokey's younger son), 72, 74, 139, 165-166, 171-172, 176
  arrival at UY Ranch, 107-111
  death, 173-174

Index

death certificate, 55
education, 111
named after Sol L. Nichols, 184
Smokey's death, 187
See also Nichols, Esther McGraw
Nichols, Smoky, 83
See also Nichols, Earl Willard "Smokey"
Nichols, Sol L. (Solomon or Saul), 75, 187
name explained, 184
Nichols, William (Smokey's brother), 177
Nichols, William Henry (Smokey's father), 55, 71, 182
Nicknames among cowboys, 28
North Sunday Creek, 33, 38, 41, 77, 79, 88, 114, 167, 176, 182
location of UY Ranch, 71, 83

— O —

O'Fallon Crick, 16
Ogden, Utah, xv
O'Hearn (judge), 140
"Old High Pockets" Titus, 27
See also "High Pockets" Titus, O.W.
"Old-Timer"
day clerk at Miles City Hotel, 37-39
Olmstead, Anna (Smokey's sister), 168, 187
O'Reilly, John Boyle, 168
Orr, Rebecca Parker, 168
Oswego, Montana, 176
Outriders, 111, 114

— P —

Paragon, Montana, 149
Parker, O. N.
family open house, 88
Parker Ranch (Hawaii), 183
Petrie, George E., "Old Man" (father of Mrs. Denny M. Smith), 39, 41-42, 45, 50
death, 151
Petroleum County, 173
Phoenix, Arizona, 114
Power, Thomas C., 78
Pyle, Don R., 114, 174

— R —

Rafter T. Ranch, xv
Ranchers, xii
Randolph, Mrs. Hugh
See Nichols, Honora (Nora, Bub's daughter)
Range Rider Reps, 180, 182
Ranger Riders, Inc., 65
Rattlesnake Creek, xiii
Red Water River, 176
Reed, J. W., 133
Reid, Margaret, 152, 170
"Retrospection" (poem), 179-180
Roberts, George, 86
Roberts, Sam "Goo", 83, 85
Rockford, Illinois, 176
Roosevelt, Theodore ("Teddy"), 22, 38
acquainted with Smokey, 67
Rosebud County, 151
Roswell, New Mexico, 178

— S —

Sacramento, California, 173
Sacramento Valley, 171
Sacred Heart Church, 173
Sadie
See Smith, Mrs. Denny M. "Sadie"
San Francisco, California, xv, 171, 179
San Francisco State College, 171
Schlichting, Al, 179, 187
Schultz, Paul, 138
Schultz, Mrs. Paul, 138
Schwabenthal, Mrs. Ernest, 179
Scotland, 85
Shaffer, F. A., 136
Sheepraising
as established industry, 135
Shoots, Martha (Smokey's mother), 55
"Shorty," 60-61
Sis
See Griffith, Elsie Cather "Sis"
Sioux City, 176
Smith, Denny M., 44, 51, 58, 165, 186
and John McLean assault case, 130, 132-133
arrested on theft, 77
purchase of Hyde Hotel, 140, 149
Smith, Mrs. Denny M. "Sadie," 37
and Carrie's move to the Dixons', 81

angry at Denny, 58
at Carrie's first meeting with Smokey, 53-54
bulk, 44
cooking, 53-54
death of father, 151
filth, 59, 64
first name unknown, 186
friendly relations with Carrie restored, 133
innuendo, 61
obscenity, 59, 64
opinion of Arneberg youngsters' father, 50
purchase of Hyde Hotel, 140
rage, 43
reading Carrie's mail, 56-57, 64
resentment toward Carrie, 56, 59
responsive to compliments, 58
rudeness, 42
showdown with Carrie, 63-65
snoring, 45
tantrums, 50
threatening Carrie, 64
Smith, Stanley, 135
Smokey
  See Nichols, Earl Willard "Smokey"
Smokey River (source of Smokey's name), 71
Smoky River (source of Smoky's name), 70
Sol, 183
  See also Nichols, Saul F. "Dutch" (Smokey's younger son)
Songs
  "Cowboy's Lament," 19
  "Gal with the Balmoral, The," 60
  "Old Chisholm Trail, The," 22
  "Red River Valley," 30
Sources
  See Documentation
South Sunday Creek, 38, 88, 149, 168
Spring roundup, 14-25, 30, 80
Stockgrowers, 144
  and homesteaders, conflicts between, 78
Stockgrowers' Association
  annual convention, 37-38, 156
Stockmen, x

Stockraising, 87
"Stone Shack" post office, 77, 131
Stout, Tom, 87
Sunday Creek, x, 156, 176, 184, 186
Sunday Crick school, 34
Sunburst, Montana, xi

— T —
Taylor Grazing District Law, 176
Telephone, 151
XIT (Ten-in-Texas) Ranch, xii
Theft
  of cattle and horses, 78
Thompson Creek, 149
Timber Creek, xiii, 38
Titanic, 22
Titus, O. W.
  "Old High Pockets," identity, 28
Titus sheep ranch, 14
Tongue River, 37, 177, 188
12-Mile Bridge, 184
12-Mile Bridge Road, 49
Twelve-Mile Bridge Road Ranch (the Dixon homestead), 63
Truscott, Al, 133, 139
Truscott, Guy, 83

— U —
UY Ranch, xv, 53, 81-82
  acquired by Smokey, 56
  and drought of 1919-1920, 155-161
  brand, 69-70
  declining fortunes, 149
  disposal of, 170
  established, 71
  hospitality to wayfarers, 107
  known as Rafter T Ranch, 149
  location, 83, 139
  size, 72, 116, 140

— V —
Van Lanningham, George (alias Jack Logan), 138
Vandervoort, Mrs. (Worden's mother), 5-8, 17
Vandervoort, Worden, 5, 14, 17, 22, 120, 123
  sweetheart Peggy, 6-7
  wife Peggy, 117

Vandervoort, Peggy, 117, 121, 122, 123, 127
   reveals Sis's deception, 118-120
Violence in the 1910s, 77

— W —

Wallace, M. H., 139, 167
Warren, Lee, 76
Warren, Mrs. Erna B., 75
Welch (judge), 133
Wells, Hugh R., 151, 176
West Fork, xii
Western Life, x, xiii, 18, 50
Westmore, Montana, xiii, 3-4, 115, 171
Wibaux, Montana, 75
Wild Horse Law, 174
Willard, Frances, 68
Wilson, Woodrow, 138
Winter of 1916-1917, 135-138

Winter of 1918-1919, 151
Women
   careers, 29
Woodburn, Oregon, 177
Wool prices, 151
"Woolies" (sheepgrowers), 78, 129
Wynes, C. N., 133
Wynne, Emmett, 75

— Y —

Yellowstone River, 37-39, 65, 85, 87, 136, 138, 147, 149, 176
Yerrington, J. E., 138
Yerrington, C. M., 138
Yuall Creek, 83, 136

— Z —

Zecker, Mr., 147
   See also Becker, Abe

Other Western American history titles
available from
Sunflower University Press®

AMERICAN FARM TOOLS: FROM HAND-POWER TO STEAM-POWER, by R. Douglas Hurt

HARVESTING SHADOWS: UNTOLD TALES FROM THE FUR TRADE, by H. D. Smiley

THE DREAD OF PLENTY: AGRICULTURAL RELIEF ACTIVITIES OF THE FEDERAL GOVERNMENT IN THE MIDDLE WEST, 1933-1939, by Michael W. Schuyler

THE RISE OF THE WHEAT STATE: A HISTORY OF KANSAS AGRICULTURE, 1861-1986, edited by George E. Ham and Robin Higham

and

The WESTERN STUDIES SERIES

Reprints in book form of theme issues of JOURNAL of the WEST — illustrated quarterly devoted to Western history and Culture.

Write for complete Sunflower University Press Catalog.

Sunflower University Press®
1531 Yuma (Box 1009)
Manhattan, Kansas 66502-4228 USA
913-539-1888